Eyewitness Accounts of the American Revolution

Letters
of Joseph Jones
# of Virginia
1777-1787

Edited by Worthington Chauncey Ford

The New York Times & Arno Press

Reprint Edition 1971 by Arno Press Inc.

*

LC# 77-140862
ISBN 0-405-01253-5

*

Eyewitness Accounts of the American Revolution, Series III
ISBN for complete set: 0-405-01187-3

*

Manufactured in the United States of America

LETTERS

OF

JOSEPH JONES

OF VIRGINIA.

———

1777–1787.

———

WASHINGTON:

DEPARTMENT OF STATE.

1889.

*

NOTE.

FEW details of the life of Joseph Jones are accessible, although he appears to have played a part by no means unimportant in Virginia politics during and subsequent to the Revolution. He was born in Virginia in 1727, and appears in the colonial House of Burgesses as a representative of King George County. At the outbreak of the war he was a member of the Committee of Safety, and in 1776 served in the Virginia Convention. One year later he represented the State in the Continental Congress, resigning to accept the position of judge of the General Court (January 23, 1778), a position that he filled for more than a year (till October, 1779). From 1780 to 1783 he served in Congress, and at a later date appears to have taken an active interest in continental and State affairs, without holding any political appointments. He was a member of the Virginia Convention in 1788, and accepted an appointment to the bench in 1789. His death occurred October 28, 1805.

The interest of Judge Jones' letters lies mainly in the careful picture he gives of the condition of Virginia politics subsequent to the treaty of peace with Great Britain. The importance of that State in deciding the course of federal events of that time can hardly be overestimated; and the struggle of internal factions over such questions as the grant of the impost, the cession of western territory to Congress, the payment of British debts, the commercial polity of the States, and finally the steps that led up to the Federal Constitution, are not only of great interest in themselves, but of vital importance as showing on how little incidents the fate of the Confederation at times depended during these most critical years of constitutional development, if the term may be applied to a period when experience was framing in a definite form what were the rudiments of an instrument of government. The same contests occurred in other States, but nowhere were they conducted with such intense bitterness, or with such an array of talent on both sides, as in Virginia. The correspondents of Judge Jones were men of note, the leading spirits of the day; and his position, from its being somewhat outside of the actual scene of strife, was advantageous for forming a judicial, though by no means unbiased opinion on the current events, as he was a strong partisan. During the administration of Washington he naturally sided with the Jefferson faction, which, mainly under the influence of the foreign relations of the States, soon developed into the Republican party, and became

iv

recognized as such after the retirement of Edmund Randolph from the Cabinet had left no representative of the opponents of the Federalists in the council of the President.

The letters printed in this volume are principally from Judge Jones to Madison, and are given for publication through the kindness of their possessor, Mr. F. B. McGuire. I have added a few others found in the Washington and Jefferson collections deposited in the Department of State, and a small number of letters from Washington and Madison to Jones. In the Gouverneur manuscripts there is a remarkable series of letters from Jones to Monroe, of which two are printed in Mr. Gilman's sketch of Monroe's life; but these manuscripts are at present not open to examination. Short notes are given where they may aid to an understanding of the text.

A number of letters from Madison to Jones are printed in the first volume of "The Papers of James Madison" (edited by Henry D. Gilpin), and for the convenience of the reader the dates and subject matter are here noted, with the pages of volume in which the letters may be found:

Page.

Philadelphia, 19 September, 1780 51
    Discussions in Congress on Mr. Jones' resolutions; the Vermont affair.

Philadelphia, 17 October, 1780... 53
    Action of Congress on the clause relating to Indian purchases; military news.

Philadelphia, 20 October, 1780... 55

> Uneasiness occasioned by the disappointment of foreign suc-
> cors; gloomy prospects for the army in winter; a remedy
> suggested.

Philadelphia, November, 1780.. 60

> The Vermont business; new arrangement of the army.

Philadelphia, 14 November, 1780 61

> State emissions of currency the bane of every salutary ar-
> rangement of the public finances; defensive condition of
> the magazines; inroads of the enemy into New York.

Philadelphia, 21 November, 1780 62

> Suggestions for legislation in Virginia; depreciation of State
> emissions; the policy Virginia should pursue relative to a
> territorial cession.

Philadelphia, 25 November, 1780.. 64

> Instructions to Mr. Jay, relative to the Mississippi claims of
> Spain; difference of opinion on the subject between Mr.
> Madison and his colleague.

Philadelphia, 28 November, 1780 67

> Suggests the liberation of slaves to make soldiers; has in-
> closed to the governor a copy of the act of Connecticut
> ceding her territorial claims to the United States; the as-
> sociation of merchants in fixing the depreciation likely to
> prove salutary.

Philadelphia, 5 December, 1780... 69

> Letters received from Mr. Jay and Mr. Carmichael, their
> tenor, and the advice of the Georgia delegates in conse-
> quence.

Philadelphia, 12 December, 1780.. 72

> Colonel Laurens appointed Envoy Extraordinary to France;
> Mr. Laurens in captivity; M. Sartine removed from the
> Navy Department and the Marquis de Castries appointed ·
> his successor.

Page.

Philadelphia, 19 December, 1780.. 76
    Regrets that the Assembly had not taken up the subject of
    the Western lands in time to have the result communi-
    cated to the Legislature of Maryland before their rising,
    and that so little progress had been made in levying
    soldiers.

It will be noticed that the letters are confined to a single year, but the subsequent communications appear to have been lost. Writing to Monroe, in 1820, Madison said: "My correspondence [with Judge Jones] ran through a much longer period, of which I have proofs on hand; and from the tenor of the above letters, and my intimacy with him, I have no doubt that my communications were often of an interesting character. Perhaps the remaining letters, or a part of them, may have escaped your search." (*Works*, III, 188.)

WORTHINGTON C. FORD.

WASHINGTON, *January, 1889.*

vii

CONTENTS.

1777.

Page.

August 11. — JONES TO WASHINGTON..   1

    Recruiting in Virginia — high bounties hurtful.

September 14. — JONES TO WASHINGTON..   2

    Asks about phaeton.

September 17. — WASHINGTON TO JONES..   2

    Reply to question about phaeton.

September 30. — JONES TO WASHINGTON..   3

    Phaeton — Virginia recruits — suggests seizure of hostile property —
    the right of retaliation.

1778.

January 22. — JONES TO WASHINGTON   5

    Resignation accepted — cabal against Washington — drafts of Vir-
    ginia — French forces in the West Indies — election of delegates to
    Congress — phaeton — Washington's letters to committee.

1780.

April 19. — JONES TO MADISON   8

    The confederation and Mississippi — supplies for the army — personal
    matters.

May 23. — JONES TO WASHINGTON...   9

    Suggests that General Weedon be given employment — affairs in the
    South.

May 31. — WASHINGTON TO JONES..   11

    Necessity of increasing the powers of Congress — disintegration of
    the confederation — General Weedon.

June —. — JONES TO WASHINGTON.. 12

Financial distress in public service — Congress has surrendered too much power to States — plan for assuming powers — caution of members — measures for aiding and increasing the army.

June 30. — JONES TO JEFFERSON.. 15

The British in the South — Sir Henry Clinton's proclamation — scheme of finance in Virginia Assembly — cession of Western lands — awakening of people — dependence on France — affairs in the West Indies — action at Springfield — scale of depreciation for loan office certificates.

July 18. — JONES TO WASHINGTON.. 19

Promotion of Colonel Morgan — objections raised — action postponed — Washington's letter to Colonel Harrison on French affairs — British at New York — the scheme of finance and drafts.

August —. — JONES TO WASHINGTON 21

Relations with France — French fleet in the Indies — operations in the South — General Greene's refusal to act as quartermaster-general — his injudicious conduct — Pickering appointed — his qualifications — Morgan's rank.

August 13. — WASHINGTON TO JONES.. 24

Greene's resignation and proposition of Congress to suspend him from command — dangers of such a step — position of the officers.

September 6. — JONES TO WASHINGTON.. 27

Report on Greene — waste of money in departments of the army — attack against New York — land cession.

October 9. — JONES TO MADISON.. 30

Question before Congress — independence of Vermont — money matters — French reinforcements — personal matters.

October 2. — JONES TO WASHINGTON.. 32

Medical department — spirit of party in Congress — the confederation and land cession.

October 2. — JONES TO MADISON.. 34

Land cessions — civil departments — appointments in medical department — finance — personal.

October 17. — JONES TO MADISON.... 37

Capture of André — personal.

October 24. — JONES TO MADISON.. 38

Military operations in the South — delegation to Congress — the French fleet.

Page.

November 5. — JONES TO MADISON.. 40

Delay in forming a house — finance scheme of March 18 — certificate system — heavy taxes and public distress — military operations.

November 10. — JONES TO MADISON 43

Paper money called in, and new emission probable — capture of British spy — operations in the South — personal — delegates' accounts.

November 18. — JONES TO MADISON.. 46

Operations in the South — bounty for negroes — finance — supplies for army — personal.

November 25. — MADISON TO JONES.. 50

Instructions to Mr. Jay — the navigation of the Mississippi — controversy with Spain — suggestions as to revising instructions.

November 25. — JONES TO MADISON.. 53

Raising drafts — dependence of South on Virginia — movements of British — funding scheme — appointment of judges — delegates' accounts.

December 2. — JONES TO MADISON.. 57

Bounties for recruits — taxes — delegation to Congress — British movements — personal.

December 5. — MADISON TO JONES.. 60

Negotiations with Spain.

December 8. — JONES TO MADISON.. 62

Continental recruits — negro scheme — its dangers — condition of Southern army.

1781.

January 2. — JONES TO MADISON.. 65

Special messenger to Congress from Assembly — personal — removal of Sartine.

January 17. — JONES TO MADISON.. 67

Ravages committed by British — continental forces in opposition — measures of Assembly.

February 21. — JONES TO WASHINGTON 68

Dr. Lewis and his parole — operations in the South — arrival of John Paul Jones — appointment of Robert Morris as superintendent of finance.

February 27. — JONES TO WASHINGTON 70

Cornwallis and Greene — the articles of confederation — reinforcements to the South.

Page.

April 3. — JONES TO MADISON.. 72

Engagement between British and French fleets — personal — British
forces in the South.

May 16. — JONES TO WASHINGTON.. 74

British in Virginia.

May 31. — JONES TO WASHINGTON.. 76

Position of the marquis — European movements — necessity of greater
activity.

April 16. — JONES TO JEFFERSON... 77

Completion of confederation — its defects — need of some coercive
power in Congress — assumption of power by that body proposed —
punishment of civil officers.

June 20. — JONES TO WASHINGTON... 80

Reinforcements for the South — need of cavalry — Harrison on Tarle-
ton's raid at Charlottesville, and unpopularity of Steuben.

July 3. — JONES TO WASHINGTON... 84

Operations in the South — militia.

August 6. — JONES TO WASHINGTON... 85

British in Carolina — European situation — admission of Vermont.

1782.

May 21. — JONES TO MADISON.. 87

Financial matters — drain of specie to the North — personal — recruiting — Conway's motion.

June 25. — JONES TO MADISON.. 90

Letters intercepted — delegates to Congress — Western territory —
personal.

July 1. — JONES TO MADISON... 92

Personal — scarcity of money.

July 8. — JONES TO MADISON... 93

Personal — French army — seizure of tobacco ship.

July 16. — JONES TO MADISON.. 95

Movements of French army.

July 22. — JONES TO MADISON.. 95

Petition of Williamsburg — military news.
xii

February 27. — JONES TO WASHINGTON 97

> Finance scheme in Congress — impost — difficulties met — public
> creditors — rumored combinations in army — the Vermont ques-
> tion — attitude of Virginia — influence of Washington — half pay to
> officers — prospect of peace.

May 6. — JONES TO WASHINGTON.. 103

> Scheme of finance — disbanding the army — Carleton and evacua-
> tion — claims for negroes.

May 25. — JONES TO MADISON.. 105

> Taxation in Virginia — delegation in Congress — impost measure —
> commerce with Great Britain — memorial of officers — Carleton's
> conduct — personal.

May 31. — JONES TO MADISON.. 109

> Finance — suspension of taxation — memorial of Virginia line — to-
> bacco bill — citizen bill — Carleton and negroes — Baylor's cavalry.

June 8. — JONES TO MADISON... 112

> Revenue scheme — attitude of delegates — election of delegates to
> Congress — land grants to officers — cession to Congress — opinion
> of people — State debt — Illinois country — English affairs — citizen
> bill.

June 14. — JONES TO MADISON... 116

> Scheme of finance — impost — land cession of Virginia — deranged
> condition of public affairs — citizen bill.

June 21. — JONES TO MADISON... 120

> Debtors' bill and British debts — continental revenue — cession of
> Virginia — pay of the army — the definitive treaty — refugees.

June 28. — JONES TO MADISON... 123

> Revenue measure — seat of government — British subjects.

July 14. — JONES TO MADISON 126

> Removal of Congress to Princeton — need of firmness in Congress.

July 21. — JONES TO MADISON... 128

> Return of Congress.

July 28. — JONES TO MADISON 129

> Treaty of commerce with Great Britain — mutiny of troops — dignity
> of Congress insulted by Philadelphia.

August 4. — JONES TO MADISON... 130

> Personal matters.

Page.

October 30. — JONES TO MADISON.. 132

    Congress and the Western country — commutation plan in the East — personal.

December 21. — JONES TO JEFFERSON... 133

    Cession to Congress — navigation law.

December 29. — JONES TO JEFFERSON... 135

    Cession of Western territory — grant of the impost — commerce with Great Britain — British debts and the treaty — confiscation act.

1784.

February 28. — JONES TO JEFFERSON... 138

    British debts — periodical payments — interest — confiscated property.

1785.

March 30. — JONES TO MADISON... 141

    Election of minister to England — foreign affairs — treaty with Indians — personal.

June 12. — JONES TO MADISON... 143

    Potomac navigation — personal — Harrison's election — Congress and the regulation of commerce.

June 23. — JONES TO MADISON... 145

    Potomac improvement.

1786.

February 21. — JONES TO JEFFERSON... 146

    Tucker's pamphlet — port bill — circuit courts — commercial policy of Great Britain — British debts — tobacco sales.

May 30. — JONES TO MADISON.. 148

    Overcrowded courts — the attorney-general — Madison's trip to the North and proposed land purchase.

1787.

June 7. — JONES TO MADISON... 150

    Constitutional convention — Lee suggests purchase of continental securities by State — question of indents — the Kentucky country.

June 29. — JONES TO MADISON.. 153

    Indents and sales of tobacco — rescue of vessel from searcher.

July 6. — JONES TO MADISON 155

    Wythe's resignation and the vacancy in the convention — Massachusetts' policy — tobacco sales.

July 23. — JONES TO MADISON.. 156

    Continued session of convention — tobacco sales — taxes in tobacco.

xiv

CORRESPONDENCE OF JOSEPH JONES.

JONES TO WASHINGTON.

PHILADELPHIA, 11 August, 1777

DEAR SIR,

Capt. Monroe * leaving town this evening I cannot avoid informing you by him that as far as his conduct has fallen under my observation, and I have not been unattentive to it, he has been diligent in endeavoring to raise men; but such is the present disposition of the people of Virginia neither Capt. Monroe or any other officer preserving the character a Gent^n ought to support can recruit men. Some men have indeed been raised, but by methods I could not recommend, and I should be sorry he should practice. The enlisting men for the usual bounty is now, and will I expect be for some time, impracticable; if at any time it should mend, on account of the high bounty given by the militia exempts, a mode of raising men very hurtfull I conceive to the recruiting business. I wish Cap^n. Monroe could have

---

* Elizabeth, the sister of Joseph Jones, married Spence Monroe, and was the mother of James Monroe, the captain of this letter, who was afterwards President of the United States.

made

1 *

made up his company on his own account, as well as that of the public; but I am satisfied any further prosecution of the attempt will be equally unsuccessful with his past endeavors. It is probable I may have the gratification of seeing you in this city as I cannot think the enemy mean to carry on their operations to the southward. A few days will I expect open their designs.

JONES TO WASHINGTON.

14 September, 1777

DEAR SIR,

Being in want of a light phaeton I directed my servant to inquire about the city for one. He tells me he has found a single light carriage which belongs to you, and has been lying here for some time. I have not seen it, but from his account of it, expect it will answer my purpose; and if you choose to sell, will purchase and give any price you may think it reasonably worth. If it is your inclination to keep it and get it out of the way of the enemy, I will take it to Lancaster, if we are obliged to move there, which you will please to determine by a line.

WASHINGTON TO JONES.

YELLOW SPRINGS, 17 September, 1777

DEAR SIR,

I have been favoured with yours of the 14th. I do not wish to sell my phaeton, but shall be happy if you will take and use it 'till I shall have occasion for it. This I request you to do, as you will thereby accommodate yourself and serve me at the same time.

JONES TO WASHINGTON.

30 September, 1777.

DEAR SIR,

I have your phaeton here though I was obliged to send for it after I left Philadelphia, being put to the route the night I received your letter. The bolt that fastens the pole-part of the long reins was lost, some brass nails also gone, and the lining much dirtied and in some places torn. I will get these little matters repaired, and have the carriage and harness kept clean and in as good order as I can, which is the least I can do for the use, though I would rather buy it if you are not determined against selling, and submit the price to yourself or our friend Col. Harrison, who may view it and pay the cash upon demand to your order. The harness, I observe, is not matched, though the difference is not very striking. Whether this happened at Philadelphia since you left it there, or before, you can judge.

We have met upon the road many companies of Virginia militia, and more are coming, though I am informed numbers are gone back, in consequence of your letters respecting those unarmed. I observe they are in general bare of clothing, which, if possible, should be furnished them, and their stay at camp made as comfortable as circumstances will admit, that when they return home they may not go disgusted, spreading evil reports greatly to the prejudice of the recruiting service and the cause in general. These men come far to support the rights and property of an invaded state, that makes little or no exertions in its own defence, but on the contrary affords every succour and support to the enemy; and rather than they should want necessaries or any other part of the army at this and the approaching inclem-
ent

ent season, I would not scruple to take all such necessaries from the disaffected wherever found. Our friends are stripped by our enemies wherever they go, and our foes freely furnish them what they want. What the last have left useful to the army I would take, and where the first are so exposed to the enemy as that what necessaries they have must unavoidably fall into their hands, I would demand a surrender of them, paying the value or giving certificates assigning the reason of such proceeding. The enemy subsists their army at our expense, drawing supplies from around them as they pass. I would subsist our army from around it as far as possible, and in the route of the enemy. These are my private sentiments, which I communicate without reserve, to be regarded or disregarded by you as you shall judge best. I own to you this conduct would hurt my feelings, as I am satisfied in many instances it must yours; but where I am satisfied the public good would result from the measure, I should endeavor to stifle those emotions of humanity and tenderness for individual distress, which in different circumstances would claim my attention and benevolence. In times like the present, and in situations like ours, rigour to internal foes is absolutely necessary, and I think has been too long delayed. To friends I would afford every possible support and protection, to Tories and equivocal characters I would yield the measure meted by the enemy to our friends. I think this is the general sentiment of our body, and of almost every Whig I converse with. How far you can prevail on yourself to carry them into execution your own feelings must determine. The right of retaliation cannot be disputed, and it is equally just and wise to benefit ourselves of those

necessaries

necessaries which it is probable, should we neglect to do so, may advantage the enemy. In pursuing this line, individuals may suffer hardship, but it is a sacrifice our friends should willingly make to the general good. Please excuse these loose thoughts. I offer them with freedom. You are equally free to disregard them. Success and happiness attend you.

Gibson's battalion came in to-day. They are but thin.

JONES TO WASHINGTON.

WILLIAMSBURG, 22 January, 1778.

DEAR SIR,

On my return to Congress I found the Speaker's letter informing me my resignation was accepted by the House of Delegates, and that I might, as soon as I pleased, return home, which I did after staying about a week to put the business we had been sent upon to camp in a proper train, the issue of which I had then every reason to expect would be according to the wishes of the army.* But what the event has been I have not yet been informed. Many reasons pressed me to retire from Congress, and if I felt a concern, it was only that in case I continued, I might possibly be of some use in obstructing or endeavoring at best to prevent, the mischievous consequences of those base arts and machinations, that are but too prevalent among some

---

*On November 28, 1777, Congress appointed a committee to repair to the army, and "in a private confidential consultation with General Washington, to consider the best and most practicable means for carrying on a winter's campaign with vigor and success, an object which Congress have much at heart." Robert Morris, Joseph Jones, and Mr. Gerry constituted the committee, and made their report December 18.

people,

people, and which it is the duty of every good man to re-
sent and suppress. I knew not so much of these matters
before I went to camp as I discovered there, and after my
return; for it was on my return only that I had the first
intimation given me of the conduct and language of a certain popular Pennsylvanian,* lately appointed to the new
Board of War, of the disposition and temper of another
gentleman of that Board, whose name the fortunate events
of last fall, hath greatly exalted I had before heard.† But
whatever may be the design of these men, and however
artfully conducted, I have no doubt but in the end it will
redound to their own disgrace. You stand too high in the
public opinion to be easily reached by their attempts; and
the same equal and disinterested conduct, the same labor
and attention, which you have manifested in the public
service from the first of the contest, will shield and protect
you from the shafts of envy and malevolence. There may
be instances, and these your good sense will point out to
you, which require your notice, and the public welfare may
be injured if passed over in silence; but in all other respects
such petty-larceny attacks, as these may be called, deserve,
as they will ever meet, your contempt.

Two thousand men are ordered to be drafted to fill up our
battalions, and five thousand volunteers raised to join you,
and serve for six months; also a State battalion in the room
of Mathews', taken by the enemy; and the counties where
draughts were deficient the last fall are ordered to make
them good, besides their proportion of the new levy. Col.
Braxton has a letter of the 17th last month from Capt. Cham-

* Mifflin.
† Gates. The "Conway cabal" is intended.

berlaine

berlaine in one of the French islands, informing him that 6000 French troops were then in the pay of Spain, that about the like number were daily expected; that the Spaniards had at Hispaniola about 10,000 men and 12 ships of the line, and it was imagined by some they meditated an attack upon Jamaica. Mr. Chamberlåine may be, as I suspect he is, equally sanguine with Mr. Bingham.

Every exertion is made use of to get a supply of provisions for the army. We are this day to choose a Delegate to Congress to serve from 10th of May to 11th of August, as R. H. Lee was chosen only to that time, and as some thing [*think*] he ought not to be longer continued, as he will then have served three years. Mr. Mercer is the other gentleman proposed.

I am sorry to hear it is probable the enemy have got possession of Mr. Pleasants' portmantua, as there were letters of Col. Harrison's to you and myself in it, and containing some things I should wish them not to know.

Having left my chair with Greentree in the city to be sold, and not having been able yet to provide myself with such a one as would suit me, I am obliged to make use of your carriage until I do. I shall send it to Mt. Vernon as soon after I am provided as lies in my power. As I am pretty confident I could rely on Col. Bannister and Mr. Harvie respecting the conduct and secrecy of any business I should mention to them, it may perhaps be in my power to be useful to my country by communications to them of any matter you may think necessary, and which you may conceive to have been neglected or not duly attended to. In this or any other matters wherein I may be possibly useful, pray exercise your pleasure with freedom.

P. S.

P. S. The letters you delivered the Committee were called for by Congress; being in my possession they were by order of Congress delivered. How the members got informed the letters were in our custody, I know not, unless from Mr. G——y,* as he and myself were the only persons of the Com: in town, and I never mentioned them to any person. But he, as a member of the Com: wanted them to be referred to in the report and of course produced.

JONES TO MADISON.†

19 April, 1780

DEAR SIR,

I must Request you will so far oblige me as to enclose me every week Dunlap's paper, or either of the others containing anything worth reading. Mr. Dunlap told me he would furnish you with the paper for me. I must also request you to send me the monthly Journals as soon as printed and such information of the proceedings from time to time as you may think necessary. Particularly be pleased to inform me of the state of the resolutions left on the table when I came off respective the Confederation and the objections that governed the House, if any of them are rejected. I should also be glad to know whether the report respecting the Mississippi has been considered. Mr. Hill told me he would not forget to propose to the Committee of the Admiralty the ordering the frigates to sail in and scour the Chesapeake Bay. I fear it was forgot, as they have not yet done it and the enemy's armed vessels still swarm here. In return for your communications, I shall from time to

---

* Mr. Gerry.

† Madison had been chosen to Congress March 4, and had reached Philadelphia on the 18th.

time

time give you whatever may be new and worth mentioning. The recommendation to the States for filling up the deficiencies in the Army and laying up in time the necessary magazines, if not already [done], should be despatched and forwarded without delay. I did not get the copy of the Report passed the day before I came away respecting the cession of the back Lands. Pray send it me and the resolutions, if passed.

Pray present my compliments to the worthy Mistress and Gentlemen of the family at the house the corner of Fifth street in Market street; to the old Lady if she is returned, and inform me whether my friend the General, and *his Friend* Buckley have finished the dispute, and whether there is any hope for the old Lady's getting rid of her plague.

P. S. From Wilmington I inclosed you a Letter for Genl Washington wch I omitted to leave with you for the I also had two letters from Col. Meade for Fitzhugh; left them behind I think, as I cannot find them—if they are found pray inclose them. Griffin requested me to send you the Letters with compliments to Walker & Bland.

JONES TO WASHINGTON.

23 May, 1780

DEAR SIR

Col. Grayson has mentioned to me his receiving a letter from Genl. Weedon* desiring to serve in the northern

---

*General Weedon had been permitted to retire, to retain his rank, and be called into service whenever an opportunity should arise (resolution 15 August, 1778). On June 14, 1780, the Board of War decided to order him to the Southern Department, to be under the command of Gates.

army,

army, if any employment can be carved out for him. This Gentleman for whom, as an officer, I entertain a regard, has attributed the regulation of his rank, which has occasioned his retiring, in great part to me; tho', God knows, I did no more in the matter than was my duty, by moving in Congress that the dispute be referred to a board of General Officers. He has ever since his return, kept himself aloof from me. About this, I have no concern. I promised Col. Grayson I would mention the proposal to you, and had no doubt, if a place could be found for him, you would call him into service. His only objection, it seems, is his serving under Woodford. If you shall find an opening for Gen'l Weedon, I believe it will be agreeable and convenient to him; but I request it may not be known to him that I had any concern in the business.

Various letters from the southward received yesterday, mention the enemies assaulting our lines at Charles Town on the 25th last month, and were repulsed with the loss of 300 killed, and from 150 to 250 prisoners. This account though by various communications originates with the postmaster at Edenton. Col. Blaine shewed me a letter received yesterday from Col. Forsyth at Richmond, in Virginia, dated the 16th mentioning that a Col. Henderson had come out from Charles Town the 28th ult°., when no material change had happened except the loss of Col. Parker of our line, by a random shot. General not without and under him about 400 light infantry, some horse and about 1,500 militia; provision in the garrison till July; 4,000 N. Carolina militia ordered down, but no arms, for which a Major Eaton had come to Virginia, and was the bearer of the news brought by Henderson. A bill had been twice
read

read for sending 2500 militia from Virginia. Thus far these accounts. If any assault had been made the 25th, it would have reached N. York, and you would have heard it ere now.

———————

WASHINGTON TO JONES.

MORRISTOWN, 31 May, 1780.

DEAR SIR,

I have been honored with your favor in answer to my letter respecting the appointment of a committee, with two others of later dates. Certain I am, unless Congress speak in a more decisive tone, unless they are vested with powers by the several States competent to the great purposes of war, or assume them as matter of right, and they and the States respectively act with more energy than they have hitherto done, that our case is lost. We can no longer drudge on in the old way. By ill timing the adoption of measures, by delays in the execution of them, or by unwarrantable jealousies, we incur enormous expenses and derive no benefit from them. One State will comply with a requisition of Congress; another neglects to do it; a third executes it by halves; and all differ either in the manner, the matter, or so much in point of time, that we are always working up hill; and, while such a system as the present one or rather want of one prevails, we shall ever be unable to apply our strength or resources to any advantage.

This, my dear Sir, is plain language to a member of Congress; but it is the language of truth and friendship. It is the result of long thinking, close application, and strict observation. I see one head gradually changing into thirteen.

I see

I see one army branching into thirteen, which, instead of looking up to Congress as the supreme controlling power of the United States, are considering themselves as dependent on their respective States. In a word, I see the powers of Congress declining too fast for the consideration and respect, which are due to them as the great representative body of America, and I am fearful of the consequences.

Till your letter came to hand, I thought General Weedon had actually resigned his commission; but, be this as it may, I see no possibility of giving him a command out of the line of his own State. He certainly knows, that every State that has troops enough to form a brigade, claims and has uniformly exercised the privilege of having them commanded by a brigadier of their own. Nor is it in my power to depart from this system, without convulsing the army, which at all times is hurtful, and at this it might be ruinous.

JONES TO WASHINGTON.

[In June, 1780.]

DEAR SIR,

I have your favor of the 31st ult°. in answer to my several letters, and was then impressed and still feel great anxiety on account of our public affairs. The present distress is to be ascribed in great part to the resolution not to issue any more bills of credit before a sufficiency of money was provided, and supplies secured for the army. Had proper precaution been taken in these matters, and the new scheme of finance been ready for the public consideration, the determination not to increase the quantity of money and the alteration introduced by the new system would not have been

been so sensibly felt, or occasioned the distress in the several Departments they have produced. From these I think we are nearly emerging, as the new money is coming into use in the several states, and will probably greatly relieve us. But by these and several other proceedings Congress have been gradually surrendering, or throwing upon the several States, the exercise of powers they should have retained, and to their utmost have exercised themselves, until at length they have scarce a power left but such as concerns foreign transactions; for as to the army, the Congress is at present little more than the medium through which the wants of the army are conveyed to the States. This body never had, or at least in few instances ever exercised, powers adequate to the purposes of war; and such as they had, have been from embarrassments and difficulties frittered away to the States, and it will be found, I fear, very difficult to recover them. A resolution passed the other day desiring the States to inform us what they had done upon certain requisitions for some time past, that we might know what we had to rely on. This may probably serve as a basis for assuming powers, should the answers afford an opening. Other resolutions are now before us. By one of them the States are desired to give express power for calling forth men, provisions, money for carrying on the war for the common defence. Others go to the assumption of them immediately. The first I have no doubt will pass this body, but will I expect sleep with the States. The others I believe will die where they are; for, so cautious are some of offending the States in this respect, a gentleman the other day plainly told us, on a proposition to order some armed vessels to search the vessels going out, to prevent the exportation

tion of flour, that if an embargo was laid in the Delaware as in this State, he consented to the measure; otherwise he never would agree to such exercise of power.

The merchants bankers in this city are making generous exertions to procure and send forward to the army a supply of flour, and will afford us great help in that article. The Massachusetts delegates read us letters whereby it appears their State have raised 4,000 men for the army and are embodying 4,000 more to be ready, if wanting. Gates, Weedon and Morgan, are ordered to the Southern department; 5000 militia are required from Virginia to join that army, and 3600 to be held in readiness; from N. Carolina 4,000, and two thousand to be held in readiness. 2500 of the Virginia militia were to march yesterday. By our accounts it would seem that States are somewhat roused from their slumber, but have rejected the scheme of finance of the 18th March last, which I fear will have a bad effect on the credit of the money of the other States that have agreed to the measure. Governor Jefferson has transmitted us a state of the Virginia troops taken from the last returns, by which it appears we have in the different corps 4000 men in service to the 30th September, and for the war or longer period than the 30th September next, including those captured in Charles Town. This surprises me, but the fact appears to be so, and where they are, or what has become of them is strange. I cannot inform you whether our legislature have ordered a draught to fill up the deficiencies, as we have no mail this week from the southward, it stopping at Annapolis for want of a rider to bring it to this place, the late rider having quitted the business.

JONES TO JEFFERSON.

PHILA: 30th June, 1780.

DEAR SIR,

The troops left by Sir Henry Clinton in South Carolina, amounting to about 3500 men besides 1500 sent to Georgia, cannot be sufficient, unless increased by the accession of Tories, to overawe that State, especially when the inhabitants shall find themselves supported by the regulars and militia going to their assistance. The 5000 militia recommended by Congress to be raised by Virginia to join the southern army, including the 2500 then or about to be raised, and the additional body to be kept in readiness. If your intelligence corresponds with the above state of the enemy's strength, it cannot now be necessary, the requisition being made upon a proposition a much greater force would have continued in South Carolina. The alteration of circumstances will justify alteration of measures, and by lessening the drafts of militia increase the number of recruits for the regular army upon which, and not upon militia, is our great dependence. Besides the calling forth, if it can be safely avoided, such large bodies of militia, lessens the productions of the earth and generally produces great distress to a number of families. Sir Henry Clinton's proclamation exempting the inhabitants of S. Carolina not taken in the town from their paroles, evince his design and expectation of gaining the people to his side, and that they will take up arms in support of the British government. It is not improbable his threats and promises may, in their present unsupported situation, induce many to do so, unless the approach of the American troops shall afford them

hopes

hopes of protection, in which case I am inclined to think he will be disappointed, as the people cannot but feel resentment at the sudden transition from assumed lenity to a demand of bearing arms in manifestation of their loyalty, or being exposed to confiscation of property and punishment for supposed enemies.

We hear our Assembly are about to reconsider their determination respecting the scheme of finance recommended by Congress, and that it was expected the measure would yet be adopted. I am happy to hear it, being confident the rejection of the proposition and the emission of more paper money could not fail of producing the worst of consequences. Let us not depart from the determination not to increase the quantity. That resolution has already appreciated the money, and a steady adherence to the measure will at length effectually do it. The present is the season for accomplishing the great work of confederation. If we suffer it to pass away, I fear it will never return. The example of New York is worthy of imitation. Could Virginia but think herself as she certainly is already full large [enough] for vigorous government, she too would moderate her desires, and cede to the United States, upon certain conditions, her territory beyond the Ohio. The act of New York, the instructions of Maryland to their delegates, and the declaration of the State upon the subject, and the late remonstrance of Virginia, are now before a Committee, and I expect they will report that it be recommended to the States having extensive western unappropriated claims, to follow the example of New York, and by law authorize their delegates to make the cession. I some time past sent Mr. Mason a copy of the New York act.

Gloomy

Gloomy as the prospect of our affairs has been and in fact still is when compared with the objects we have in view through the course of this campaign, I yet feel myself revived by the accounts lately received from our State, that the people are at length awakened from their slumber and appear to act with becoming spirit and order at this important conjuncture, especially as the States in general, for the present moment seem to be roused and impressed with the necessity of great and immediate exertions; and if the spirit is kept up for a while we may reasonably hope for the happiest consequences. I have been much and still am depressed to think that America should do so little for herself while France is proposing to do so much; that she should, contending for everything dear and valuable to her, look on with folded arms and suffer other powers almost unassisted by us, to work out our salvation and independence. The idea is humiliating; the fact must be dishonourable, and our posterity will blush to read it in future story.

Letters from Martinique, so late as the 3^d and 4th of this month, inform us of the arrival of a Spanish frigate announcing that 12 Spanish ships of the line, 4-50 gun and six frigates, with about 10,000 troops, were about 200 leagues to windward when the frigate left them, coming forward to join the French fleet and forces. The Count Guichen was going out with 16 sail of the line to meet them. Upon the junction of these fleets, the superiority of the combined force will be decided, and we may expect soon to hear of some important stroke made in that quarter. It was conjectured their first attempt would be St. Lucie, if the approach if the hurricane months did not discourage the enterprise. Then Jamaica, and from thence come

2 *

come round and by uniting the whole forces, sweep the coast of North America. The   is grand and opens so pleasing a prospect to us, I will not lessen your pleasure by a doubt of it being verified. These letters further inform us that the armament carrying on at Brest, and which they expected was for the West Indies, is for North America, and that it was expected to sail about the 15ᵗʰ April. It is said to consist of ten ships of the line and a large body of troops. No doubt they will make it as large as they well can, as it is evident the war will be principally here and in the West Indies. Between the 12ᵗʰ and 19ᵗʰ of last month, Rodney and Guichen have had three engagements; the last a severe action in which the Count kept the sea. For further particulars I refer you to the inclosed paper, as well as for the account so far as we are yet informed of the action at Springfield in the Jerseys, between our troops and militia under Genˡ. Greene and the British and Hessians under Knyphausen. The Jersey militia acquired immortal fame, as indeed they do upon almost every occasion when they are engaged with the enemy.

Congress have formed the scale of depreciation to apply to Loan Office certificates:

from the 1ˢᵗ Sepᵗ 1777 to 1ˢᵗ March, 1778, at........................... 1$\frac{3}{5}$
thence to Sept. 1ˢᵗ '78.. 4
thence to March 1ˢᵗ '79... 10
thence to Sept 1ˢᵗ '79... 18
thence to March 18ᵗʰ '80... 40

The intermediate time of the respective periods to be calculated in geometrical proportion. The resolves will be immediately published. This will reduce the principal of loans from 46,559,235 to 11,053,573.

JONES TO WASHINGTON.

PHILA: 18 July, 1780

DEAR SIR,

A report from the Board of War in consequence of a letter of General Gates to Congress, referred to the Board, respecting the promotion of Col. Danl. Morgan* to the office of Brigadier General, now lies upon the table, at my request. The Board have stated his former services, his being first colonel of our line, and the deficiency of that state at present in her quota of troops. If a promotion of general officers is to take place, and to be made through the line of the army, Morgan has many before him; but if the promotions are to be made through the line of the State, that officer it appears stands first. General Gates has mentioned his intention of giving Morgan the command of a body of light infantry, but as the state has given the command of the militia lately sent to the southward to Col. Stevens, who was Morgan's junior officer in the Continental line, with the commission of Brigadier General, he will command Col. Morgan, and this Gates thinks, will disgust him, and therefore with great earnestness and warmth presses his promotion. I shall thank you for your confidential communications upon the matter, as the report, I think, will not be pressed or taken up until the Virginia delegates are fully informed, as it was upon my motion to obtain time for information, it lies upon the table. Besides, as he left the army in disgust under your immediate command, I

---

*Morgan had resigned in 1779 because the command of the light infantry had been given to another, but received a furlough until he might be called into service. On June 14, 1780, the Board of War recommended that he be sent to the southward to serve under Gates, and later endorsed the suggestion of Gates to give him a commission as brigadier-general. Congress so ordered.—*Journals*, October 13, 1780.

did

did not like the present mode of his obtaining the promotions without that I know of any alteration of circumstances, at the pressing instance of General Gates. Pray, my dear sir, do you recollect the purport of a letter lately writte.. to Col. Harrison, speaker of the Delegates, representing the deranged state of the French finances; their as well as Spain's declining navy, and the increasing strength of the British navy. I have heard of such a letter that gentleman received from you, and had shewn it to many of the members of our Assembly, and that it was like to prejudice rather than promote the service.* I mention this in confidence, as the purport of the letter may have been misrepresented, and I have it not directly from one who saw it or heard it read. Between ourselves, I fear that worthy man is no zealous friend of the Alliance. I may be mistaken, but it is my present opinion.

An account transmitted to the Admiralty Board by General Foreman makes the British on the N. York station, nine line of battle ships, two or three fifties, and 17 frigates and other armed vessels. Should this intelligence be true, the French fleet as we have been told (though we have not yet the particulars of their strength) will be unequal to the undertaking. My letters from Virginia speak of our people as being roused. A bill had passed the Delegates by a majority of 3 only adopting the scheme of finance recommended by Congress; thirteen of the senate only were present, the opinion of ten of these publicly known — five for and five against the bill. It was conjectured the others were in favor of the measure. Every 15th militia man is to be

---

* This letter was probably of the same purport as that from Washington to Joseph Reed, May 28, 1780, printed in Sparks' "Writings of Washington," vii., 58.

drafted

drafted to fill up the deficiency of our line; this bill was also before the senate. I hope you find the recruits coming in fast; the news of the arrival of the fleet will accelerate them.

JONES TO WASHINGTON.

[August, 1780.]*

DEAR SIR,

Your letter to Col. Harrison turns out as I expected before I received your full information. If the whole had been read and attended to, it was impossible to put any other construction on your manner of treating the subject than to convince your correspondent of the absolute necessity of great exertions this campaign, while we had a promising prospect before us, lest by remissness and delay we should find our ally, as well as ourselves, embarrassed with greater difficulties than at present; and I very sincerely wish, should this summer pass away without some signal advantage gained on our part, we may not find your conjectures verified in event. I have my hopes we shall yet be able to do something important upon the arrival of the French reinforcement, as I presume their fleet will then command the water, without which, I confess, I have no sanguine expectations. With the command of the water, the enterprise may be successful. Mr. Bingham has received a letter from Martinique informing him the combined fleet fell to leeward on the 5th. July, supposed for Jamaica — thirty-three or thirty-six ships of the line and

---

* Probably the 6th. On the 5th Pickering was chosen quartermaster-general in place of Greene, and on the 7th his acceptance was communicated to Congress. Jones writes before that acceptance was known.

12,000

12,000 troops. They expected a reinforcement of a few thousand troops more. If this account be true, it is probable Jamaica will fall and that we may have them along our coast.

You are desired by some late resolutions to turn your thoughts towards the recovery of S. Carolina and Georgia, as soon as the operations of the campaign in this quarter have been executed.* Gates' and De Kalb's letters represent the distresses of the Southern Department in a very gloomy light as to provisions and equipments. The Virginia recruits, when raised, are ordered to join that army. If this interferes with your plans, you should let us know it, as they will not be ready to march until the beginning of next month. The law passed by the legislature will probably bring into the field about 3,000. A Colonel or Major Pinckney of South Carolina, writes Col. Motte, a delegate of that State, that the enemy are not more than 2500 strong at their ports in the country, exclusive of horse, of which they have a strong corps, and about 800 or 1000 men in Charles Town. Of our 2500 militia, not above 1500 had reached Hillsborough in N. Carolina; but Mr. D. Jameson of the Virginia Privy Council writes us that many of the deserters had been taken up and sent forward to Hillsborough. Caswell had about 1200 militia under him; Baylor's and Bland's dragoons nearly equipped; so that if they can get provisions sufficient and forage, which by this letter it is probable they are furnished with, they will be in condition to face the enemy, and I hope drive them into the town.

* Journals, August 5, 1780.

We

We have been greatly perplexed the last week with General Greene's refusal to act in the office of Quarter Master
General, unless the new system was totally repealed, and
he was allowed to conduct it under your direction in such
manner as he thought most conducive to the public service;
besides, Congress were to *request* Pettit and Cox to resume
their offices.   If General Greene thought the new system
wanted amendment and had pointed out the defect, Congress would have considered the matter, and I doubt not
would have made the necessary alteration.   But the manner of these demands, made in such peremptory terms, at
the moment of action, when the campaign was opened, the
enemy in the field, and our ally waiting for co-operation,
has lessened General Greene not only in the opinion of
Congress, but I think of the public; and I question whether
it will terminate with the acceptance of his refusal only.
On Saturday, Col. Pickering was appointed to the office of
Quarter Master General, with the rank of Colonel and the
pay and rations of a Brigadier-General, and to hold his
place at the Board of War without pay or right to act while
in the office of Quarter Master General.   This gentleman's
integrity, ability and attention to business, will I hope not
only prevent the evils to be apprehended from a change in
so important a department at this time, but will I hope be
able to reform some of the abuses crept into that business
and lessen the amazing expenditure of the department.   He
must, if he accepts, have a disagreeable office in the present
state of our finances, but we must support him all we can.
    The promotion I mentioned has not taken place, though
if we take up the business, I suppose it will be done, as M.
is the oldest Colonel and Gates is the only Major General
                                                  belonging

belonging to Virginia, and the State has a right to two. But I see no occasion of stirring in it at present, as if taken up, it must be upon the general principles of promotion, and then not only Virginia but Maryland and other States will expect to partake of the same privilege of bringing forward their officers, when I believe, there are few States whose lines are so full as to justify the promotions.

WASHINGTON TO JONES.

HEAD-QUARTERS, TAPPAN, 13 August, 1780.
DEAR SIR,

The subject of this letter will be confined to a single point. I shall make it as short as possible, and write it with frankness. If any sentiment therefore is delivered, which might be displeasing to you as a member of Congress, ascribe it to the freedom which is taken with you by a friend, who has nothing in view but the public good.

In your letter without date, but which came to hand yesterday, an idea is held up, as if the acceptance of General Greene's resignation of the quartermaster's department was not all that Congress meant to do with him. If by this it is in contemplation to suspend him from his command in the line, of which he made an express reservation at the time of entering on the other duty, and it is not already enacted, let me beseech you to consider well what you are about before you resolve. I shall neither condemn nor acquit General Greene's conduct for the act of resignation, because all the antecedent correspondence is necessary to form a right judgment of the matter; and possibly, if the affair is ever brought

brought before the public, you may find him treading on better ground than you seem to imagine; but this by the by. My sole aim at present is to advertise you of what I think would be the consequences of suspending him from his command in the line (a matter distinct from the other) without a proper trial. A procedure of this kind must touch the feelings of every officer. It will show in a conspicuous point of view the uncertain tenure by which they hold their commissions. In a word, it will exhibit such a specimen of power, that I question much if there is an officer in the whole line, that will hold a commission beyond the end of the campaign, if he does till then. Such an act in the most despotic government would be attended at least with loud complaints.

It does not require with you, I am sure, at this time of day, arguments to prove, that there is no set of men in the United States, considered as a body, that have made the same sacrifices of their interest in support of the common cause, as the officers of the American army; that nothing but a love of their country, of honor, and a desire of seeing their labors crowned with success, could possibly induce them to continue one moment in service; that no officer can live upon his pay; that hundreds, having spent their little all in addition to their scanty public allowance, have resigned, because they could no longer support themselves as officers; that numbers are at this moment rendered unfit for duty for want of clothing, while the rest are wasting their property, and some of them verging fast to the gulf of poverty and distress.

Can it be supposed, that men under these circumstances, who can derive at best, if the contest ends happily, only the advantages which accrue in equal proportion to others, will
sit

sit patient under such a precedent? Surely they will not; for the measure, not the man, will be the subject of consideration, and each will ask himself this question; If Congress by its mere fiat, without inquiry and without trial, will suspend an officer to-day, and an officer of such high rank, may it not be my turn to-morrow, and ought I to put it in the power of any man or body of men to sport with my commission and character, and lay me under the necessity of tamely acquiescing, or, by an appeal to the public, exposing matters, which must be injurious to its interests? The suspension of Generals Schuyler and St. Clair, though it was preceded by the loss of Ticonderoga, which contributed not a little for the moment to excite prejudices against them, was by no means viewed with a satisfactory eye by many discerning men, though it was in a manner supported by the public clamor; and the one in contemplation I am almost certain will be generally reprobated by the army.

Suffer not, my friend, if it is within the compass of your abilities to prevent it, so disagreeable an event to take place. I do not mean to justify, to countenance, or excuse, in the most distant degree, any expressions of disrespect, which the question, if he has used any, may have offered to Congress; no more than I do any unreasonable matters he may have required respecting the quartermaster-general's department; but, as I have already observed, my letter is to prevent his suspension, because I fear, I feel, that it must lead to very disagreeable and injurious consequences. General Greene has his numerous friends out of the army as well as in it; and, from his character and consideration in the world, he might not, when he felt himself wounded in so summary a way, withhold himself from a discussion, that could not

at

at best promote the public cause. As a military officer he
stands very fair, and very deservedly so, in the opinion of
all his acquaintance. These sentiments are the result of my
own reflections, and I hasten to inform you of them. I do
not know that General Greene has ever heard of the matter,
and I hope he never may; nor am I acquainted with the
opinion of a single officer in the whole army upon the subject, nor will any tone be given by me. It is my wish to
prevent the proceeding; for, sure I am, that it cannot be
brought to a happy issue, if it takes place.

JONES TO WASHINGTON.

PHILA: 6 September, 1780

DEAR SIR,

I have received your favour of the 13th ult°. upon the
subject of a report respecting a certain gentleman, and
thank you for the freedom and candid manner of your
communications. The resentment discovered against the
gentleman alluded to began to subside before your letter
came to hand, and though for some time it was occasion-
ally mentioned in conversation, it has lately died away, and
will I expect not be revived. The report of the committee
not only accepted his resignation, but went further, and I
believe had it been then determined, the gentleman would
have been informed his services in the line of the army
would have been dispensed with, that he might have leisure
to attend to the settlement of his accounts. Had this step
been taken, it is probable a resignation would have ensued
and perhaps a public discussion in the papers, which could
have produced no good; and upon the whole I am well
pleased

pleased the matter was carried no further than it has been. But unacquainted as I am with antecedent circumstances, and judging from what was before me, my opinion was the gentleman was justly reprehensible for the manner of his conduct as a servant of the public, employed as an important officer, or as a citizen, embarked in the common cause of America. The amazing sums of money gone into that department under his superintendance, about eighty millions, and it is said, about thirty millions unpaid, the whole of which is unaccounted for, have excited uneasiness not only in this body but the people at large, who call out for a settlement of the public accounts. And although repeated endeavours have been used to bring the officers in the great departments of the army to account, none have been rendered nor any likelihood of bringing them to a settlement. The embezzlement and waste of public property in these departments have greatly contributed to enhance our debt and depreciate the currency, and these abuses demand inquiry and punishment; but I see no fair prospect of obtaining satisfaction for past transgressions and shall be happy to find we shall be able to avoid the like practices in future. A reform or an attempt to reform seemed absolutely necessary for the satisfaction of the public, and although the new system was pronounced a physical impossibility in execution, others who have served long in the army and were of the committee that made the alterations, entertained a contrary opinion, and they affirm the gentleman now in office, if he can be supported with money, can fully carry the new system into execution. In short, I have seen some, and have been told of so many abuses in the Q. Master's Commissaries' and Medical departments in the course of the last

two

two years that I candidly confess I feel a degree of resentment against the conduct of many in those departments bordering on prejudice so nearly that I have resolved to condemn no person even in opinion without clear proof of delinquency, lest I should injure the character of some honest men in the general censure which unhappily is but too prevalent.

What I feared for some time is at length but too evident, that our designs against New York must wait for more favourable circumstances to attempt carrying them into execution. Perhaps something may in the course of the winter be done to the south. Should we be in a situation to recover our losses there and be in time provided with a well appointed regular army and magazine of provisions laid up, it is to be hoped we shall in the spring before the enemy can be reinforced and obtain supplies, be in a condition to act offensively against New York. Your letters of the 20th last month and the 27th circular to the States, are before a committee and will in a day or two be reported upon as to flour and meat. The great objects of drawing forth in time a competent regular army and laying up magazines will soon come in and I hope soon go through Congress, that the several states may proceed to make the necessary provisions. I shall leave this place on Thursday for Virginia and mean to attend our next session of Assembly in hopes of promoting a cession on the part of the state of their claim to the lands to the N. W. of the Ohio to the United States, which will be recommended to all the States having unappropriated western territory for the purpose of completing the Confederation. I shall be glad to hear from you while there upon any matters that may occur and you shall think proper to communicate.

JONES TO MADISON.

SPRING HILL 9th Octr. 1780

DEAR SIR,

I think you acted very prudently in declining to press on the part of Virginia the Resolutions I left for the consideration of Congress. Had I been present, I should have done the same, as I had no intention when they were offered that Virginia should appear anxious about them. Whatever my opinion might be as to their propriety or justice, I meant to leave them to the candor of Congress and to those impartial reflections which might ever, and upon such great questions I trust will, generally, govern their Councils. I wished also to feel the pulse of that Body upon these points and to know the reasons that governed their resolutions; that if the resolutions were any of them rejected and the ground upon which they were overruled good. The Assembly of Virg^n. might in their deliberation on the subject perhaps be influenced by like considerations. I thought I could discover a strong propensity among some of the members to give independence to the people of Vermont. This affair ought to be a warning to Congress how to act in similar situations in future. To be remiss and indecisive upon such pretensions as these, serves only to support and not discourage the claimants. It does more it shews the weakness or wickedness of Government and must ultimately produce dishonor and contempt. I have sent forward your letter to the auditors and inclosed my account whereby the balance due to me is £3000 which I have directed to be applied to your use and requested the money might be forwarded to you as speedily as possible as I well knew you wanted it.

The

The fourth of the eight thousand pounds drawn for is included in the three thousand pounds, and so I have informed the auditors; so that when Meade's orders are paid you must take on my account two thousand pounds. Out of M^{rs}. House's account of 8000 some odd dol^s. is to be deducted what I advanced for wine — 5 s hard money overpaid at the former settlem^t and the money advanced by me for the family, the amount of which I gave you in the first instance and M^{rs}. Trist in the second. I shall go off to Richm^d. if M^{rs}. Jones gets wholly well ab^t the middle of next week, from whence you shall regularly hear from me. Have no reasons been assigned by the Minister for the disappointments respecting the reported reinforcement. If there are any that are worthy notice I should be glad to be furnished with them that I may do justice to the good intentions of France and to their exertions in the common cause, which some are but too apt to suspect upon the present occasion, and though I am not among the number I must confess I am at a loss how fully to satisfy the doubts of some and to silence the insinuations of others who ground their observations upon the transactions of the present year, and particularly the promised reinforcements. I have mentioned this matter in confidence to you that if you think it proper you may take occasion to intimate to the proper persons, how much it would contribute to the satisfaction of the friends of the alliance to be able to give some satisfactory reasons for our disappointments, not only of the aid to come to the Continent, but of our expectations of advantages to be obtained over an enemy by the combined forces in the W. Indies — in short their inactivity there as well as in Europe. These I know are delicate matters, but they are

such

such as we ought to know, as well for our future government, as for silencing those who throw out insinuations injurious to France.

Be pleased to present my compliments to Mr. Pleasants and inform him he shall receive an answer from me respecting his house soon after my arrival at Richmond, which I expected, would be the beginning of this month from the usual time of the Assembly's meeting; but their adjourning to a later day has prevented my doing it so soon as I intended. In the meantime will you be pleased to sound Mr. Pemberton as to his house, and the terms if he is inclined to let it with stable room for four horses, a chariot house, garden and small pasture, with such furniture as he can spare. This information I shall thank you for as soon as possible. The report here is that Congress has suspended Gates from his command until his conduct is inquired into. Our recruits I am told are going on to the southern camp; our militia, I believe, are returned, and another division is I understand preparing to take their place. Compliments to the delegation.

JONES TO WASHINGTON.

VIRGᴬ 2 October 1780.

DEAR SIR,

The Medical Department was under the consideration of a committee before I left Congress and will, it is probable, undergo a change that may curtail the number of the present appointments. Should this be the case, and the new arrangement take place before I return (which at present it is my intention to do before Christmas) I shall recommend

to

to the support of the Virginia delegates the gentlemen you have been pleased to mention, whose long services and well known characters intitle them to be among the first officers in the establishment.

If I am not mistaken, the spirit of party is much abated in Congress. Some instances of the old prejudices and partialities that disgusted and must ever disgrace their councils I think have been discovered; but they are few, and I entertained hopes the flame was nearly extinguished. And although some restless tempers, as some there are, and ever will be in public assemblies of men, may attempt to revive these disputes, which were carried to such height between the contending factions as to neglect the more important concerns of the public, there are I trust a sufficient number of mild spirits who will oppose and repress such dishonourable attempts and confine themselves to the discussion alone of such matters as justice and the general welfare require. I am certain the important objects now before Congress are sufficient to engage their attention and employ their time without perplexing themselves by a revival of old and expiring controversies. It was with reluctance I left Philadelphia before the report upon your letter respecting the army and magazines was complete, and the arrangements of the civil officers of Congress were digested; but an apprehension that the Assembly was to meet the first Monday in October as usual, and a desire of spending a short time with my family before I went to Richmond, determined me to set out so as to reach home about the middle of September. I now find I might have stayed a fortnight longer, as the session does not commence until the third Monday in this month. Congress having taken some steps towards completing

3 *

completing the Federal Union, which I anxiously wish to accomplish, induced me to be here early in the session, that the sense of this State upon that interesting question might be taken. That if the proposition was approved, it might be divulged to the other States without delay, and Virginia being more interested than any other in a cession of unappropriated territory, the example would not fail to have weight, and be followed by others. We are already too large for the energy of republican government, and I fear shall be so if the Assembly shall relinquish their claim to the northwest of the Ohio, to the Continent. I wished too to be [at] the beginning of the session to urge the filling up our battalions immediately, and providing magazines in time, as the ensuing winter to the south and the approaching spring to the north, if our ally shall command the water, might afford us favourable opportunities of acting to advantage. But alas! instead of the French commanding the water, we have the mortification to hear Rodney, with 12 ships of the line and four frigates, has arrived at the Hook. Where, for God's sake, is Count Guichen with his great and formidable fleet? surely, not inactive.

JONES TO MADISON.

2 October, 1780.

DEAR SIR,

I thank you for your favor of the 19th ult. and the inclosures. It was really a mortifying circumstance to find the French Fleet converted into twelve British ships of the line and four frigates from which nothing can effectively relieve us but the arrival of a superior number of French battle ships.

ships.   And unless these come I fear many of our people
not only here but in other States will entertain unfavourable
opinions of the ability at least, if not the inclination, of our
ally to give us effectual support.   The alteration of ye resolutions I left are not I think material excepting the one postponed, not to be taken up, which I am certain will be made
a condition by Virginia in any cession she may make, as
there are jealousies entertained of certain individuals greatly
interested in that question.   Congress cannot in honor or
justice delay their determination on the Vermont dispute.
Had the Territorial claims of New York and N. Hampshire
been settled in the first instance, the step of Vermont would
not at this day, have been known.   Delay has given them a
name and made them formidable.   Such excrescences should
be taken off on their first appearance, as then the work is easy
and less dangerous than when they have grown to a head.
We know not what may be the consequences if Congress
shall countenance by precedent the dismembering of States,
because the people blown up into discontents by designing
ambitious men shall ask or demand it; fix the boundaries
of these States and let the people who live within their respective limits know they are their citizens and must submit
to their Government.   I was one of a Committee to whom
the General's long Letter on very important matters was referred.   We had come to some resolutions before I left Congress but no Report made.   Pray inform me what has been
done, and whether any recommendation has gone to the
States to fill up their Battalions immediately and lay up
magazines in time.   I was also of a Committee to arrange
or reform the civil departments of Congress, and it was in
contemplation to place at the head of the Foreign Affairs,
                                                              the

the Admiralty, and Treasury, some respectable persons to conduct the Business and be responsible. Has any thing been done in these matters, they are important and should not be forgotten. We shall never have these great departments well managed until something of this kind is done. I cannot forget Mr. L——l's* very *candid* confession respecting Dr. Franklin's complaint of want of information of our affairs. Is there a Report made respecting the medical department, and is there any hope of getting that branch reformed? If any removals are to take place and persons shall be wanting to fill the higher offices of that department, there are two gentlemen mentioned to me who from their long and faithful services deserve the attention of Congress. I mean Dr. Craik and Dr. Cochran. Col. Mason wrote to us about Mr. Harrison in case a Consul should be wanting for Spain. I have since received a letter from Col. Meade upon the same subject and have assured him should any such appointment take place Mr. Harrison should be recommended but there was no reason to expect this would soon be the case. This reminds me of the report respecting the Mississippi—what has been done with it?

Has Dr. Lee made his appearance and does he attempt to revive the old disputes? Would not the publication of extracts of the several acts of the States that have adopted the Scheme of Finance, specifying the Funds established for support of redemption of the money, be of use? As the money is to circulate through all the States, all the States should be properly and fully informed of the solidity of the Funds. Much, very much, depends on our supporting the credit of the new money.

---

* Lovell.

The

The Assembly adjourned to the 3ᵈ Monday of this month instead of the first, their usual time of meeting. Had I known it I might have staid a week or two longer with you. I have heard nothing of Mr. Henry and cannot inform you when he intends to Congress. I found Mrs. Jones and my little Boy in bad health when I got Home. She has been so ever since July, and still in a low state. He is something better though not quite well. I shall prevail on her for her Health' sake if nothing else to visit the north next spring if I do so myself of which I shall soon inform you and give you the trouble of securing either Mr. Pemberton's or Mr. Pleasant's House, as she will not take the small pox by inoculation, and by living in the country she may avoid it.

We have a report that the French Fleet is arrived at Newport. I hope for a confirmation of it by the post to-morrow. Make my compliments to Genˡ. Scott and the other gentlemen of the family of my acquaintance. Also to the good lady of the house.

JONES TO MADISON.

VIRGᴬ· 17ᵗʰ October, 1780.

DEAR SIR,

We must place the taking Col. Andre among the fortunate occurrences during the present war. A more wicked and ruinous combination could hardly have been formed if the accounts published in the papers are generally true; and the three honest militia men, who rendered us the service should be rewarded.

An attack early the last week of the ague and fever will prevent my being in Richmond until next Sunday; at which time

time I determine to be there, if my family's and own health will permit. We have suffered more sickness this fall in Virginia than was perhaps ever known. There is scarce a family at this late season but are part of them sick, and one remarkable symptom of which all complain of is a constant sickness of the stomach and loathing of almost everything offered them. This is found to be obstinate and difficult to remove. I hope you continue well and that the family are so.

N. B. I forgot to mention and recommend to your attention Drs. Cochran and Craik in the Medical Department, as I expect from the system's being formed the appointments will take place. These are recommended to me by a good judge of their services and qualifications.

JONES TO MADISON.

VIRGᴬ· 24 October 1780.

DEAR SIR,

I very sincerely thank you for your friendly and regular correspondence. When I am in Richmond, which I am in hopes to be the last of this week (being sufficiently recovered from my late indisposition as to be able to take the bark), I will endeavour to make you amends by a communication from time to time of our proceedings in Assembly, and such southern intelligence as may be worth mentioning.

I presume the last post carried you the account of our success against Ferguson's party by a body of North Carolina militia. It is said the news came to our Governor by express from Genl. Gates. From Richmond Genl. Muhlenberg communicated the intelligence by express to Genl. Weedon ;

Weedon; but no doubt the Governor has given the President full information. Our account was that Ferguson and 150 of the enemy were slain, 810 prisoners with a large number of arms taken. Genl. Weedon, who has hitherto remained in Fredericksburg, is now under marching orders and is set out this week; from whence I conclude there are sufficient of our new levies gone forward to give him employment and to form two brigades, as Muhlenberg being his senior, of course commands the first. I expect you will soon have Mr. Smith, to succeed Mr. Walker. I hope he will avoid entering into and reviving those party contentions that when he was in Congress before so much disgraced that body. And I trust the gentlemen of our delegation will in general check every attempt that may be made to renew former disputes, or to do anything more than what justice shall require. I own I have my fears Congress will again be drawn into sects and divisions.

What has been done with the Alliance, and what with Capt. Landais? In a former letter I wished to be informed what was the real cause of the disappointment that the 2^d [?] division of the French force did not come out; the inactive campaign in the W. Indies and the combined, or rather, the fleets of France and Spain, not combining in the British Channel. I should, if it can be obtained, be glad to hear the sentiments of certain gentlemen on these matters.

Mrs. Jones' indisposition has at length terminated in the third day, ague and fever. My little boy is somewhat better, but his mother is by a long and severe illness reduced to a skeleton.

JONES TO MADISON.

RICHMOND, 5th November, 1780.

DEAR SIR,

I thank you for your two last letters. The first I received at home, the last (Octr. 24th) found me in this place, where I have been since the 31st ult. waiting with about 64 others, members of the House of Delegates, to make a House to proceed upon business, but as yet we are eight or ten short, and I see no likelihood of the number speedily increasing, as it has not increased for three or four days. For the members who reside in the counties upon the seaboard, or contiguous thereto, some excuse may be assigned; and so there may for some of the frontier counties, from the disturbances and apprehensions of the enemy in that quarter. But I am at a loss to make an excuse for those of the interior part of the State, many of whom are still absent. This neglect of public duty is the more criminal in our present situation, which must necessarily require the exertions of the Legislature in aid of the Executive, to repel the invasion of the enemy, but it is exceedingly prejudicial to the common cause, in delaying to adopt and prosecute with becoming spirit those measures necessary for furnishing men and supplies to the Army. The late practice of granting certificates for supplies and transportation for the support of the army and the internal police of the respective States, transferable and allowed to discharge taxes, together with the late emissions of some of the States, however expedient and necessary the practice was found at the time—all certainly tend to counteract the scheme of finance of March the 18th, to increase the circulating medium and precipitate

our

our ruin.   Some course must be taken to stop the progress
of this traffic, or we never shall get the new money into circulation, as the whole collections are forestalled by certificates, auditor's warrants, &c. all which now circulate as
freely in payment of taxes as the old currency.   And when
money is paid the collectors, rather than hazard the loss of
the bad bills, readily exchange the money in the country
for certificates, whereby the treasury is almost totally deprived of money collections.

If our people, knowing the public distress, will not
forego the advantage or convenience of present payment for
their supplies, they must abide the consequences; but my
hopes are, they will submit to any regulations the Assembly
may adopt for raising either men, supplying magazines, or
supporting the credit of the currency, all of which are the
great objects we shall bend our minds to, as soon as we have
a House.   These are also the objects every other State
should seriously attend to, and in particular the putting a
stop to the circulation of the certificates, &c. you mention,
for the measure should be general.   You will therefore
oblige me with information: what steps are taking in other
States on this head; what prospects for speedily recruiting
the army and laying up magazines to the S. and middle district for the supply of the main army.   The States never
were blessed with greater plenty or had it more in their
power to lay up ample stores of provisions for the army,
than at present; and if the people will not lend them to the
public and await for future payment, they must be taken;
but they should be so taken as to occasion as little disgust
as possible, which a regular apportionment of specific articles may effect.   Some vent should be found for the surplus
                                                              of

of the earth's production or I fear the collection of heavy taxes will be found oppressive and produce clamour and discontent—if their collection shall be found practicable at any rate. Whether this can be effected by internal demand and consumption I doubt; and if it can not, no other mode will answer but opening the ports. In laying specific taxes I am inclined to think double the quantity wanted should be required from the people; as our half may be allowed for the expence of collecting, transporting, commissaries wages and the waste unavoidable, besides sometimes a total loss by water and the damage in the storehouses. These things make a specific tax less eligible than others, could it be avoided.

Letters from Muhlenberg of the 2ᵈ. which arrived this morning mention the enemy all in Portsmouth; the ships in the road; different accounts as to their fortifying at Portsmouth; certain intelligence is expected every moment from Col. Gibson, who is down with a party for that purpose; accounts from head quarters came in last night inform[ing that] 4,000 more troops had sailed from N. York southerly. A few days past we had very flattering accounts from the south (Cornwallis and his whole army in captivity). The hope of its being true, though not strong in me from the imperfections in the intelligence, has died away in every one for want of confirmation. One 64 and three frigates would have taken the whole fleet in our bay, as there are only a 44 and 2 frigates, with a 20 gun ship of Goodrich's. We have reason to think Dunlap's——* are in the hands of the enemy. Compliments to the family.

---

* Men or mail.

JONES TO MADISON.

RICHMOND, 10th November, 1780.

DEAR SIR,

I have your favor by the last post. We have had a House since Monday, and in committee of the whole this day have voted the raising the deficiency of our continental troops for the war, and to recruit them by a bounty, which I expect will be very high; but the members in general seem to prefer that method to any other, let the expence be what it will. What may be the ultimate determination is yet very uncertain, as there is no accounting for the whim and caprice of some; but from the unanimity with which the question was carried to-day (not a voice dissenting) I presage a happy issue to the business. We have recommended the bringing in the old paper currency to exchange for the new bills just arrived. By this operation, if it succeeds, we lose one-half the sum we expected to have the first use of; but of which we have been deprived by the necessity of anticipating the taxes by which channel alone the old money would come in. And now from an empty treasury and the amazing expence incurred by calling forth men to oppose and repel the invasion, and the pressing necessity for money, it will be unavoidable I fear the making a further emission, and which was also re-solved this day in committee. Every one seems to be sensi-ble of the evils of this measure, but they see or think they see, greater evils in our present situation will result to the community from the want of money than from the increase of it. And indeed I can not see a way of carrying on our operations at this juncture so indispensably necessary, with-out money. Of the evils that present themselves we think we choose the least.

On

On the fourth instant one of our light horsemen met and closely interrogated a suspected person whose conscious guilt at length manifested itself and induced the horseman to search him, when he found in his possession a letter written on very thin or silk paper from Gen^1. Leslie to Lord Cornwallis, informing his Lordship he had taken post at Portsmouth and waited his orders.* The person apprehended is it seems a citizen employed by Leslie who informs Cornwallis he was to receive a handsome reward if he succeeded in his embassy. Unfortunately for the embassador, he was in a fair way to receive the compliment of the bowstring, alias the halter, on the 8th instant. Three other fellows were apprehended yesterday about ten miles below this place; the one a sergeant of British grenadiers, the others soldiers, and all deserters from the barracks the last summer and got into New York. They were part of the British army at Portsmouth, and it is supposed were on their way to the barracks—whether sent with written or verbal instructions has not yet come out.

Our force below on each side James River must be formidable. Ten thousand of the militia were I am informed ordered out, but the draughts from several counties have been countermanded as soon as satisfactory information was obtained of the strength of the enemy. Six thousand, it is thought, will be a number very sufficient to secure us against the armament now at Portsmouth. It is supposed this party was to have attempted a junction with the army under Cornwallis somewhere in North Carolina, but our present force in the field here and the unpromising [prospects] that present themselves to Cornwallis in the south, will prove strong

* This intercepted letter is printed in "Jefferson's Works," i., 271, note.

impediments

impediments to the execution of the project. Our militia are commanded by our supernumerary and other experienced officers. Col. Lawson has a corps of about 700 Volunteer horse and infantry—about 300 of them under my nephew Col. Monroe compose part of the light infantry commanded by Col. Gibson. If the enemy stay as by the intercepted letter it would seem they mean to do, there must soon be skirmishing, if nothing more; but I hope our people will be cautious, until they are somewhat used to skirmishing, of venturing a more general action.

I enclose you an answer to Mr. Pleasants which you will be pleased to deliver, unless you can engage for me Pemberton's house upon moderate terms with coach house, stabling for four horses, and the use of a small pasture with the garden; also a hayloft and as much furniture for kitchen and house as he can spare. Pemberton's place is more convenient and would suit me rather better than the other, but is I fear not so healthy, which is a great object not only to myself but to Mrs. Jones who has this summer undergone a long and tedious illness from which she is not yet recovered, having terminated in the third day ague and fever. I know not what sort of house on the inside Pemberton's is and wish, if you are likely to engage for it, you would take the trouble of looking into the house. If his demands are unreasonable, I would at any rate take Pleasants'. You will observe I propose to pay the rent quarterly, which Mr. Pleasants required should be all paid at the commencement of the year. If he will not consent to this I will agree to pay the first quarter at the commencement and so proceed on to the first of November.

Mr.

Mr. Henry, I believe, returns to Philadelphia as I hear nothing of his intention to resign. He sent to the treasurer for £8,000 to enable him to set out, but could not obtain it. I have done what I could since I have been here to forward money to the delegates, but could not effect it. Mr. Jameson yesterday informed me they would be able speedily to send you a supply. Our accounts have not yet been before the Assembly, but expect them to-day or Monday. The account from the books should be stated and sent forward agreeable to the resolve. I shall endeavor to get matters so settled as that our supply be regular. With compliments to the gentlemen of the delegation and the family at Mrs. House's.

JONES TO MADISON.

RICHMOND, 18th November, 1780

DEAR SIR,

I have your favour by the last post and very sincerely wish the *State* news may prove true, but I cannot yet believe the Dutchmen will go to war. The Generals Greene and Steuben are here on their way to the southward. From that quarter we are destitute of intelligence, and from the army to the eastward in this State we have nothing material to mention. The enemy still at or near Portsmouth and our people at convenient distance on the south side James River, between Suffolk and Portsmouth; both parties eating their bread and beef in quiet without any quarreling that we hear of. The design that was formed to attack about 200 of the enemy at an outpost since called in, miscarried by the disagreement between Colonels Gibson and

Parker

Parker about rank—a fair and perhaps the only opportunity our people will have of striking the enemy to advantage, and which has been lost by a contention about rank. It was not so between the five Colonels whose militia united to attack Ferguson, for there the command was given to Campbell by several colonels, himself only a lieutenant colonel.

In a private committee we have gone through the outlines of a bill [to] supply the deficiency of our quota of the Continental army for the war. The[y] made a bounty of a negro not younger than ten or older than 40 years for each recruit—these to be required from all negro holders having twenty and upwards in their possession, in the proportion of every twentieth negro at such prices as [are] settled by the bill in hard money, to be paid for in eight years, the payment to commence the fifth year, with an interest of 5 ℔ ct. to go in payment of taxes. The persons furnishing the negros to be exempted from future draughts, unless upon invasion or insurrection; and if they do not by a certain period voluntarily surrender them, compulsion is to be used. This plan if it can be so digested in the bill as to appear practicable in execution, will I believe produce the men for the war, and from what I can learn, be palatable to the Delegates whatever it may be to the Senate. Strong objections certainly lie against it and the negro holders in general already clamour against the project and will encounter it with all their force. But you know a great part of our House are not of that class, or own so few of them as not to come within the law should it pass. The scheme bears hard upon those wealthy in negroes, as that property is sacrificed to the exoneration of other property. It is in
nature

nature of a loan to the state and will aid the public exigence for money, but will not, I am pretty certain, come under the denomination of the ancient mode of *benevolence*. Though determined to join in any scheme that shall be practicable for raising them for the war, I confess I am no great friend to the one I have stated, though in Committee I have given it my assistance towards making it perfect, as a majority of the committee adopted the plan. But my notion is, and I think the mode would be more just and equably certain in procuring the men, to throw the militia into divisions as by the last law, and require the divisions to find a negro of a certain value or age, or money equivalent to that value; and on failure of obtaining a recruit by a limited time, the division to be drafted with a small bounty to the soldier whose lot it may be to serve for three years. But the negro bounty cannot fail to procure men for the war under either scheme, with the draught as the *dernier resort*.

Some doubts having arisen on the construction of the law for issuing and funding the new money under the scheme of 18th March last, a bill was brought in to explain and amend it. While under consideration of a committee of the whole the speaker proposed an amendment whereby the new bills as well as those emitted by act of the last session called the 2 million act, should be a legal tender in payment of all debts, and that the last, which was not payable in taxes until twelve months hence, should now be received for taxes. After long debate the Committee of the Whole divided, when about ten appeared in favor of the amendment; so that the House and Senate agreeing to the clause, the new money of Congress and the late emission of
this

this State, and I suppose of course the emission of this session, will all be a lawful tender in payment of debts — for such is the state of things here a further emission becomes indispensable. Thus you will see the scheme of the 18th of March will be in great measure defeated by their proceedings, and not have a fair chance to produce by its vigorous execution those advantages to the public it was well calculated to effect.

The executive are pursuing vigorous courses to lay up a sufficiency of beef and we have authorized them to send a Commissary into North Carolina to concert with the executive there the laying up proper supplies of pork, as it seems the legislature of that State had prohibited the removal of that article from the State, and in Virginia there will be very little pork obtained, though I think we have plenty of beef and of every kind of grain.

Col. Lee has this moment received a line from Weedon informing him the enemy were all embarked but wherefor is uncertain. Some conjectured up James River, but as they are all on board they must mean to leave us. Can you contrive me the journals of Congress for August and September, and indeed October if printed. I mentioned in my last my terms for Pemberton's or Pleasants' house. Let me hear from you on the subject as soon as you can. Neither —— or Henry are I believe yet set out. I repeat your sending a copy of the account from the books of the delegates. These accounts are not yet laid before the House by the auditor, so that I can give you no information how they are relished. I am charged by the auditor with 2000*l* on account the 8,000*l* drawn in favor of George Meade & Co, and which you were to receive for me, but I cannot find

4 *

find by the treasurer's account that he has paid the warrants. Has the money been received by the delegates? The executive informs me a bill for 20,000*l* had been sent for the use of the delegation.

MADISON TO JONES.

PHILADELPHIA, Nov. 25, 1780.

DEAR SIR,

I informed you some time ago that the instructions to Mr. Jay had passed Congress, in a form which was entirely to my mind. I since informed you that a committee was preparing a letter to him, explanatory of the principles and objects of the instructions. This letter also passed in a form equally satisfactory. I did not suppose that anything further would be done on the subject; at least, until further intelligence should arrive from Mr. Jay. It now appears that I was mistaken. The delegates from Georgia and South Carolina, apprehensive that a *uti possidetis* may be obtruded on the belligerent Powers by the armed neutrality in Europe, and hoping that the accession of Spain to the alliance will give greater concert and success to the military operations that may be pursued for the recovery of their States, and likewise add weight to the means that may be used for obviating a *uti possidetis*, have moved for a reconsideration of the instructions, in order to empower Mr. Jay, in case of necessity, to yield to the claims of Spain on condition of her guarantying our independence and affording us a handsome subsidy. The expediency of such a motion is further urged from the dangerous negotiations now on foot, by British emissaries, for detaching Spain from

from the war. Wednesday last was assigned for the consideration of this motion, and it has continued the order of the day ever since, without being taken up. What the fate of it will be I do not predict; but whatever its own fate may be, it must do mischief in its operation. It will not probably be concealed that such a motion has been made and supported, and the weight which our demands would derive from unanimity and decision must be lost. I flatter myself, however, that Congress will see the impropriety of sacrificing the acknowledged limits and claims of any State, without the express concurrence of such State. Obstacles enough will be thrown in the way of peace, if it is to be bid for at the expense of particular members of the Union. The Eastern States must, on the first suggestion, take the alarm for their fisheries. If they will not support other States in their rights, they cannot expect to be supported themselves when theirs come into question.

In this important business, which so deeply affects the claims and interests of Virginia, and which I know she has so much at heart, I have not the satisfaction to harmonize in sentiments with my colleague. He has embraced an opinion that we have no just claim to the subject in controversy between us and Spain, and that it is the interest of Virginia not to adhere to it. Under this impression, he drew up a letter to the Executive to be communicated to the Legislature, stating, in general, the difficulty Congress might be under, and calling their attention to a revision of their instructions to their Delegates on the subject. I was obliged to object to such a step, and, in order to prevent it, observed, that the instructions were given by the Legislature of Virginia on mature consideration of the case, and

on

on a supposition that Spain would make the demands she
has done; that no other event has occurred to change the
mind of our constituents but the armed neutrality in Europe
and the successes of the enemy to the southward, which are
as well known to them as to ourselves; that we might every
moment expect a third Delegate here, who would either adjust or decide the difference in opinion between us, and that
whatever went from the delegation would then go in its proper form and have its proper effect; that if the instructions
from Virginia were to be revised, and their ultimatum reduced, it could not be concealed in so populous an assembly, and everything which our minister should be authorized
to yield would be insisted on; that Mr. Jay's last despatches
encouraged us to expect that Spain would not be inflexible
if we were so; that we might every day expect to have more
satisfactory information from him; that, finally, if it should
be thought expedient to listen to the pretensions of Spain,
it would be best, before we took any decisive step in the
matter, to take the counsel of those who best know the interests, and have the greatest influence on the opinions, of
our constituents; that, as you were both a member of Congress and of the Legislature, and were now with the latter,
you would be an unexceptionable medium for effecting this;
and that I would write to you for the purpose by the first safe
conveyance.

These objections had not the weight with my colleague
which they had with me. He adhered to his first determination, and has, I believe, sent the letter above mentioned,
by Mr. Walker, who will, I suppose, soon forward it to the
Governor. You will readily conceive the embarrassments
this affair must have cost me. All I have to ask of you is,
that

that if my refusing to concur with my colleague in recommending to the Legislature a revision of their instructions should be misconstrued by any, you will be so good as to place it in its true light; and if you agree with me as to the danger of giving express power to concede, or the inexpediency of conceding at all, that you will consult with gentlemen of the above description and acquaint me with the result.

I need not observe to you that the alarms with respect to the inflexibility of Spain in her demands, the progress of British intrigues at Madrid, and the danger of a *uti possidetis*, may, with no small probability, be regarded as artifices for securing her objects on the Mississippi. Mr. Adams, in a late letter from Amsterdam, a copy of which has been enclosed to the Governor, supposes that the pretended success of the British emissaries at Madrid is nothing but a ministerial finesse to facilitate the loans and keep up the spirits of the people.

This will be conveyed by Col. Grayson, who has promised to deliver it himself; or if anything unforseen should prevent his going to Richmond, to put it into such hands as will equally insure its safe delivery.

JONES TO MADISON.

RICHMOND, 25th November, 1780

DEAR SIR,

I have yours of the 14th and from my soul wish I could inform you we proceed with that vigour and dispatch the urgency of the public wants requires. The bill for filling up the quota of our Continental troops has not yet been

reported

reported although we have been in a Committee upon it a fortnight.   Such various opinions prevail as to the mode of raising them as well as the bounty to be given that I can hardly yet venture to say what will be the result.   I think however we shall give a bounty in negros to such soldiers as will enlist for the war, the negro not to be transferred but forthcoming if the soldier shall desert the service, and in that case to revert to the public to recruit another man in his room.   If in thirty days men are not recruited by bounty for the war, a draught to take place.   It seems to be the prevailing opinion for three years, though I expect this long period upon a draft will be opposed, but I have my hopes it will be carried for that time.   This bill will, however, go into the House to morrow or Monday.   We shall then take up finance, and I see clearly we shall totally defeat the scheme of the 18th of March last by the large emissions the urgent and present demands of the State render unavoidable, I think at least 5 M. pounds.

Almost the sole support and succour of the Southern department depend upon Virginia, and perplexed and surrounded with difficulties as we are, there yet appears among people in general a disposition to make exertions to their utmost ability, and I have my hopes we shall accomplish a great proportion, if not the whole required from us. Methods are pursuing by the executive to obtain a good store of beef, and we have directed a Commissary to go to North Carolina to concert with that government the laying up a sufficiency of pork, as that article is rather scarce here, but in much greater purity there.   The executive will be armed with powers competent to drawing forth every resource, and if we can but furnish money for transportation

and

and other contingent charges, the great specific supplies that will be furnished will I hope keep matters in a way that will not let the army suffer for want of our assistance.

The enemy have left us without leaving behind them as heretofore those marks of ravage and devastation that have but too generally attended their progress. All the unrigged vessels remain unhurt; no burnings and but little plundering, and this when done, was by the Tories in general and reprobated, we are informed, by Leslie and the Commodore as well as the principal officers of their army and fleet. Surely this sudden and most extraordinary change in the behaviour of the enemy has a meaning which, though we are yet at a loss to unfold, will ere long be made manifest. We have no late accounts from the southward. The last from Gates, Smallwood and Mason [or Magen] speak of our force being inconsiderable and almost naked and frequently without provisions. Genl. Greene is gone forward, leaving Baron Steuben here to arrange matters with the State, and then to follow him.

We have had a warm debate in the House upon a bill to explain and amend the act of the last session for funding the new bills of credit of Congress, under the scheme of the 18th of March. The question agitated, whether those bills, as well as the two million of State money issued last session, should be a tender in payment of debts; and determined that they should be a legal tender. H-n-y for the question, R. H. L. against it, and both aided by the auxiliaries, took up two days or nearly in discussing the question. Indeed we lose a great deal too much time in idle unnecessary debate.

Mr. Blair was yesterday chosen to succeed Mr. Nicholas in

in the Chancery, and to morrow we fill up the vacancy in the General Court, which I plainly see will be the lot of Mr. Fleming. I had thought of G—f—n,* but found it was in vain to propose him. I expected somebody would mention Mr. James Henry, but it has not been done. I believe that would be also, unless as you know the advantage a member has over an absent person. I this day presented [a bill] for relief to Mr. Dunlap for his loss, but am very doubtful whether it will be attended with success. I wish to hear what he says about getting another apparatus. or whether he declines the business altogether. I should be sorry he should do so, as I am certain he would be very useful to the State, and will in the end find his account in undertaking the business.

Mrs. Jones I find is not yet well of the ague and fever which, being of the third day, will I fear continue on her for some time, as it has already been her companion through the fall. The extract of your letter to the governor respecting supply of money was laid before the House, as well as Col. Bland's quere for his satisfaction upon a scruple respecting commerce. They are referred to a committee, and so are the delegates' accounts. M. M. S's† account lodged in the auditor's office, occasions speculation. You would do well, if not already done, to transmit a state of the accounts from the book, and in particular M. S., as it is said it was never examined according to custom by the delegates. This last upon second thoughts should not come alone. It will appear pointed. It would be better to get the whole transcribed by some person and pay him, charg-

* Mr. Griffin.
† Meriwether Smith.

ing

ing the State. I shall endeavour, if the matter comes on before I leave Richmond to get the delegates, supply of money fixed upon some sure and certain fund, that they may no longer be exposed to the difficulties lately experienced. R. H. Lee talks of lessening the number to save the ex pence.

JONES TO MADISON.

RICHMOND, 2 December, 1780.

DEAR SIR,

I have no letter from you by this week's post, although I expect you sent one, as Mr. Griffin informs me what news here was worth communicating, especially the contents of Mr. Adams' letter,* you had mentioned. I have been much indisposed the greater part of this week, and not able to give much assistance in the business upon hand, which is chiefly the bills for recruiting the army, and emitting and funding I suppose six millions of pounds. The first was reported to the House near a week past, and has been the subject of debate every day. It went in a plan for giving negro bounties and has been rejected by an amendment from the word *whereas*. The amendment proposes to give a bounty of five thousand pounds to each recruit for the war or three years, which is uncertain, but I expect will be the last and this money to be demanded from all persons having a possible property above 500*l* specie value at the rate of 2 p^r ct. At present it stands no lower than those having property

---

*Giving information that General Provost had sailed from England with a few frigates for Cape Fear, and that the British ministry were determined to make an active winter campaign in the Southern States. *Adams to Congress*, August 23, 1780.

above

above three hundred, but I expect it will be brought to
100*l*. The money, or some specifics which are allowed to
be paid in lieu of money, are to be collected by the last
of January. The collection, added to the tax to be paid by
the people under the act of the last session will be very
difficult for them to comply with, but the situation of the
treasury without money and the demands now due from the
public and the late expences occasioned by the invasion,
will soon exhaust the new emission, which will be gone as
soon and as fast as they can make it. For almost the whole
burthen of the southern army will and must, as Gen[l]. Greene
informs us, fall on this State. I am in hopes the bounty of
5 will be reduced to three thousand pounds, which will then
for 3000 men amount to 9,000,000 — an amazing sum for a
bounty. But our legislators are timid, or affect many of
them to be timid, about a draft which had better be made
of the militia, to serve two years without bounty, unless a
very small one, and that body or any other that may be
necessary, supplied from the militia by rotation, to be at
camp by the time the others are to come away, and to serve
other two years. In the meantime let an exemption from
draft, or even militia duty out of the State, be offered by
the law to every person who recruits a soldier for the war,
whereby a number of our people will be constantly endeav-
ouring to enlist soldiers for the war, and a great number I
have no doubt might be so enlisted for a much less sum than
the bounty proposed to be offered. If we raise the 3000
only for three years, it is intended to furnish money to the
officers or some proper person to take the proper occasion
of enlisting as many of them for the war as they can, and
there are moments when most of them may be enlisted.

It is

It is in contemplation to send some proper person to lay before Congress the resources of this State and its ability to maintain the southern war, in which embassy perhaps North Carolina may join that more dependence may not be placed on us than we are able to bear, lest a disappointment may ensue, as we have no doubt the great operations of this winter and next spring will be to the south. The person is also to press the making strong remonstrances to France and Spain for their co-operation, with proper force by sea and land, to recover S. Carolina and Georgia. A resolution to this effect now lies on the table.

Mr. Henry has sent in his resignation; no proposal yet of filling his place and am doubtful whether it will be done, as some think to save expence the number should be lessened. Our accounts, as well as those of the preceding delegates are before a committee. No step yet taken about the cession of lands, but will be taken up so soon as the recruiting and supply bills are passed. Mr. Mason has not yet appeared, and I do not expect he will this session, as he has the remains upon him of a severe attack of the gout. However, I have my hopes we shall obtain a cession of all beyond the Ohio.

Certainly if Leslie is gone to the southward and another reinforcement from New York and also one reported from England in that quarter, Congress or the commander in chief should send on to the southward the Pennsylvania line before it is too late. For if these reinforcements arrive they will go where they please, as our army will be unable to withstand them and the severity of the approaching season will retard the march exceedingly of any succour by land.

Mrs.

Mrs. Jones still continues to suffer the assaults of the ague and fever, and she writes me it has so weakened and reduced her she fears she will not be in condition to go north. If her state of health should be such as to render her unable to travel, I think I shall decline it myself. Have you fixed anything with Pemberton or Pleasants? If you have not and either of them are disposed to rent upon the terms I mentioned, endeavour to make it conditional, that if in a month or six weeks I should decline the bargain, I may be at liberty, as they should if any other offered to rent their places. As soon as I return home, or soon after, you shall hear further from me upon this subject. I send for my horses to-day, and shall return about the 10th or 12th. Your letters after the receipt of this please to direct to Fredericksburg until further informed. I have [this] moment your letters which I expect by some mistake went on to Petersburg, as this is the day for the return of the post from there. I find you have engaged Pleasants' house for me and must abide by it. I thank you for your trouble in the matter, and shall be ready to return you the favour wherever in my power.

MADISON TO JONES.

[Extract.]

December 5th, 1780.

DEAR SIR,

We had letters yesterday from Mr. Jay and Mr. Carmichael, as late as the 4th and 9th of September. Mr. Jay informs us that it is absolutely necessary to cease drawing bills on him; that 150,000 dollars, to be repaid in three years, with some aid in clothing, &c., is all that the court

will

will adventure for us. The general tenor of the letter is, that our affairs there make little progress; that the court is rather backward; that the navigation of the Mississippi is likely to prove a very serious difficulty; that Spain has herself been endeavoring to borrow a large sum in France, on which she meant to issue a paper currency; that the terms and means used by her displeased Mr. Neckar, who, in consequence, threw such discouragements on it, as, in turn, were not very pleasing to the Spanish minister; that Mr. Cumberland is still at Madrid, laboring, in concert with other secret emissaries of Britain, to give unfavorable impressions of our affairs; that he is permitted to keep up a correspondence by his couriers with London; that if negotiations for peace should be instituted this winter, as Spain has not yet taken a decided part with regard to America, England will probably choose to make Madrid, rather than Versailles, the seat of it. However unfavorable many of these particulars may appear, it is the concurrent representation of the above ministers that our disappointment of pecuniary succor at Madrid is to be imputed to the want of ability, and not of inclination, to supply us; that the steadiness of his Catholic Majesty is entirely confided in by the French ambassador; and that the mysterious conduct of Mr. Cumberland, and of the court of Spain towards him, seems to excite no uneasiness in the ambassador. The letters add, that, on the pressing remonstrance of France and Spain, Portugal had agreed to shut her ports against English prizes, but that she persisted in her refusal to accede to the armed neutrality.

The receipt of the foregoing intelligence has awakened the attention of the Georgia delegates to their motion, of which

which I informed you particularly by Col. Grayson. It has lain ever since it was made undisturbed on the table. This morning is assigned for the consideration of it, and I expect it will, without fail, be taken up. I do not believe Congress will adopt it without the express concurrence of all the States immediately interested. Both my principles and my instructions will determine me to oppose it. Virginia and the United States in general are too deeply interested in the subject of controversy to give it up as long as there is a possibility of retaining it. And I have ever considered the mysterious and reserved behaviour of Spain, particularly her backwardness in the article of money, as intended to alarm us into concessions rather than as the effect of a real indifference to our fate, or to an alliance with us. I am very anxious, notwithstanding, to have an answer to my letter by Grayson.

JONES TO MADISON.

RICHMOND, 8 December, 1780.

DEAR SIR,

I have yours of November 28th by the post, and wish I could inform you the Assembly had yet fixed the plan of recruiting our quota of Continentals, but such various opinions and modes are proposed that great delay has been the consequence. The present proposition is a bounty of 5,000 for the war, 2500 for three years if it comes to a draft for that period — the whole to be collected from the taxable property by the last of January, each division to clothe the soldier and find him a beef. It is expected this mode will raise us 3000 men and as many beeves to feed them.
Whether

Whether this will pass I cannot pretend to say, but am told it is the most agreeable of any thing that has been proposed. My speaking thus doubtfully proceeds from my non-attendance in the House this week, being confined by a slight but lingering fever. I am somewhat better to day, and hope in a few days to be in the House again, though I shall continue a very short time, having sent for my carriage to go home.

The finance bill was under consideration of the committee of the whole yesterday. I have not heard whether they got through it. This finished, the next great object will be to take up the question of ceding the back country. This I want done before I go, and also to have some mode fixed for the delegates being regularly supplied. I mean to take a few days of next week for these purposes before I set out. I have already requested your future letters to be addressed to me at Fredericksburg until I give you notice of my being about to leave Virginia for Pennsylvania. This I expect yet to do, as by the last post Mrs. Jones informs me she and my son are both upon the mend. You need not, therefore, if not already done, say anything to Mr. Pleasants, as I expect Mrs. Jones may be prevailed upon — her health being in some measure restored — to venture north.

The negro scheme is laid aside upon a doubt of its practicability in any reasonable time, and because it was generally considered as unjust, sacrificing the property of a part of the community to the exoneration of the rest. It was reprobated also as inhuman and cruel. How far your idea of raising black regiments, giving them freedom would be politic, in this and the negro States, deserves well to be considered, so long as the States mean to continue any part
of

of that people in their present subjection; as it must be doubtful whether the measure would not ultimately tend to increase the army of the enemy as much or more than our own. For if they once see us disposed to arm the blacks for the field they will follow the example and not disdain to fight us in our own way, and this would bring on the southern States probably inevitable ruin. At least it would draw off immediately such a number of the best labourers for the culture of the earth as to ruin individuals, distress the State, and perhaps the Continent, when all that can be raised by their assistance is but barely sufficient to keep us jogging along with the great expence of the war. The freedom of these people is a great and desirable object. To have a clear view of it would be happy for Virginia; but whenever it is attempted, it must be I conceive by some gradual course, allowing time as they go off for labourers to take their places, or we shall suffer exceedingly under the sudden revolution which perhaps arming them would produce. Adieu. I hope my head will be easier when I next write.

Maj. Lee is now here on his way to the south. Our army we are told is very weak in that quarter, and we hear the enemy are reinforcing from New York. I am apprehensive all Virginia can do will not be sufficient to make head against them, if it be true what is said, that they will be eight thousand strong. Clothing and blankets are exceedingly wanting in our army. For want of these not above 400 of 800 and upwards of our levies can yet go forward since the enemy left us.

JONES TO MADISON.

2nd January, 1781.

DEAR SIR,

I was not in a condition to visit Fredericksburg the last week, or you should then have been informed that Mr. Braxton has taken the warrant upon the treasurer and agreed to give bills payable in Philadelphia for the amount of 10,000*l*. Mr. Fitzhugh was to bring them up, but it is not yet arrived, unless he came yesterday, which may be the case, as Braxton wrote me it was expected they would rise on Saturday last. That, however, I think doubtful, as I am pretty certain they would if possible, take up the question of the back lands as well as the Mississippi affair with Spain.

It seems there was a ballot for a person to repair to Congress and the General, in consequence of the resolution I before mentioned to you, the day Braxton wrote, and the House having divided between the Speaker and R. H. Lee, the question could not be decided. As the Speaker being the person in question could not [vote] in his own case, after much debate and perplexity Lee withdrew his pretensions, so that Harrison stood elected. Braxton says the old fellow was so disgusted with the vote that he believed he would resign his appointment. Should that be the case I question whether any one undertakes the embassy, especially as it is in great part superseded by Col. Laurens' appointment. No doubt but the delegates in Congress by proper instructions could have done everything this agent can do, but as he is to attend the governor and our delegation thin, it was thought best to appoint some person not of the delegation, as he

would

5 *

would necessarily be absent for some time on the visit to Head Quarters. I told Mr. Henry, the father of the proposition, I had no doubt but every proper measure was already taken and that I did not believe any good would result from it, further than might be expected from the state the Commonwealth could give of its ability to comply with the requisitions of Congress ; that if more was laid upon her than she could bear some other course might in time be taken to supply what she would likely fall short, but this could be done by a representation of the matter by the Executive to the Delegates as well as in any other way.

I have not heard the issue of the report on the delegates' accounts and their future allowance. If nothing unforeseen prevents, I shall hope to be able to leave this about the 12ᵗʰ instant for Philadelphia. Mrs. Jones' third day ague and fever still pursues her, and she is so reduced as to be scarcely able to take exercise, which makes it rather disagreeable to leave her. But as she has agreed to try the northern air next spring her power and several things are wanting for housekeeping, it makes a trip on my part necessary previous to her going, as she cannot venture into the city until I could make the proper provision for fear of the small pox.

It is to be hoped the removal of Sartine* and the introduction of this new man of distinguished abilities into the management of the naval department of France, will produce a more active and vigorous prosecution of the war in favour of America than we have yet experienced. I fear from the great delays in the Assembly, our new levies will be late in the field.

---

*M. de Sartine was succeeded by the Marquis de Castries.

JONES TO MADISON.

17 January, 1781.

DEAR SIR,

I was in doubt whether to write you by this post or not, as I intend setting out in a day or two for Philadelphia, and should probably have the pleasure of taking you by the hand before my letter would arrive. But as we have yet in this quarter received no certain account of the departure of the enemy, and it is expected they intend to pay us a visit up Potomack, I may possibly delay my journey a few to see the event of this affair.

We hear they have done great injury to the houses of Col. Harrison of Berkeley, and carried away all his valuable negros. If they attempt to visit Fredericksburg, I believe they will have reason to repent the enterprise, as there now is there and in the neighbourhood a considerable force, and a further reinforcement expected to-day. I have, I confess, no expectation they will come up Potomack River. Their Force is inadequate to any attack where the country has been previously alarmed which is here and I believe in most other parts the case. If they do us any injury it must be by plundering private persons of their property along the shores and receiving the negroes who may run away and join them. It is not improbable this days post may bring us information of their departure. I have a letter from Col. Anthony Thruston for you with I presume the cash inclosed you advanced his son. The assembly have come to a set resolution relinquishing to the States the lands beyond the Ohio upon certain conditions. They have also changed the allowance to the Delegates to 46 specie ℔ day.

Be

Be pleased to renew a ticket in the lottery for Mr. H. Ballaile No. 12153 @ price of 40 doll and for J. J. the number inclosed.

JONES TO WASHINGTON.

PHILA: 21st February, 1781.

DEAR SIR,

I beg leave to mention to you a young gentleman captured by the enemy when the Buckskin fell into their hands in Chesapeake Bay, and who was put on shore under parole and wishes to be discharged from the obligation as soon as possible, as he conceives it restrains him not only from acting in the field, should the situation of his country require his services, but even from attending the hospital for his instruction, which he is very desirous of doing. The person I speak of is Dr. Jno. Lewis, a son of the late Mr. Charles Lewis, whose name I mentioned to you some years ago while he was in New York, and being refused the liberty of coming out was at length obliged to return to Great Britain. His parole is, I think, irregular, as it extends only to his not doing or speaking anything to the prejudice of the enemy, without the clause of rendering himself when called for.

You will receive from the president a copy of a report which has passed in Congress, in consequence of Col. Harrison's communications; and you will also be informed of the arrival of Provost with a reinforcement to the enemy in the south, and of his progress since his arrival. Arnold's position at Portsmouth, Provost in North Carolina, and Cornwallis in South Carolina, will I fear effectually obstruct

struct the supplies from our State, or so delay them as to render Greene's situation critical. If the French ships from Rhode Island shall succeed in their enterprise in the Chesapeake, the event will be propitious and produce the happiest effects. Our State will be thereby further aided by a supply of 5000 men, arms and some stores, retaken in and sent forward in one of the French frigates. The arrival of Provost and the great want of arms in the southern States, it must be confessed, present a rather gloomy prospect and under this temper of mind you will receive a letter reiterating what has, I think, been several times intimated, a desire that you will pay particular attention to the southern department. I wish we could but content ourselves with a communication of facts and any reflections upon them for illustration, leaving the combination and execution of the various operations of a campaign to those whose business it is to project and execute them. P. Jones's arrival gives us no relief in cloathing and arms, a disappointment the more to be regretted as our wants increase. Yet we know not whom to blame. Jones will, I expect, unfold this dark and as yet mysterious business. I presume you must have been informed that Virginia has receded from her former instructions to her delegates in Congress respecting the claim on her part to the free navigation of the Mississippi, which, if approved by Congress, will probably bring about an alliance with Spain and an acknowledgement of our independence. No doubt this event, if it takes place, will give us more credit in Europe.

We are about appointing the officers who are to be at the head of our great departments. Yesterday Mr. Morris,
without

without a vote against him (tho' S. A.* and his colleague, General W.† declined to ballot) was chosen financier. I cannot say he will accept, but have some hopes he will. Our finances want a Neckar to arrange and reform them. Morris is, I believe, the best qualified of any our country affords for the arduous undertaking. We shall in a day or two appoint the officers for the foreign affairs and the marine. I wish we had men in these offices as well qualified to execute them as Morris in the treasury. Some however that are nominated, if they can be chosen will do very well. We are under difficulties about the war office, least any person we could now put into it may answer so well as the present commissioners. This may, and I expect will, postpone that appointment.

JONES TO WASHINGTON.

PHILA: 27ᵗʰ February, 1781.

DEAR SIR,

I missed the opportunity by the express of sending you the letter of the 21ˢᵗ, which is now inclosed, as it contains a request respecting Dr. Lewis, and will serve to shew you I meant to pay my compliments to you as soon as I was certain after my arrival, you had declined your visit to R. Island. Lord Cornwallis has put every thing to the hazard, and if the people of Virginia and North Carolina have not the spirit to turn and support Genˡ. Greene under the present fair prospect of totally ruining his Lordship's army, they deserve not the blessings we are contending for. Genˡ.

---

* Samuel Adams.
† Artemas Ward.

Greene's

Greene's conduct has been judicious. Indeed from the wise measures concerted by him for the arrangement and support of the southern department and which were communicated by him to the Assembly while I was at Richmond, I entertained very favorable sentiments of that gentleman's fitness for the command of the southern army; and his behaviour since has manifested he is equal to the appointment. If he is properly supported he will give us a good account of Cornwallis. I was concerned when I came to Congress to hear so small a favor was refused Genl. Greene, then going to his new command, as that of granting his request respecting Dr. McHenry. From my conversations with gentlemen on the subject, many think the Genl. should have been indulged, and if it can be done, the question will probably be revived. This, however the Dr. should not be acquainted with, least the attempt should be unsuccessful. Thursday next is appointed for the Maryland Delegates to subscribe the Articles of Confederation, an event that cannot fail to produce happy consequences both at home and abroad. The Articles, it is certain, are defective and amendments and additional powers are necessary, and these will be and must be speedily proposed to the States for their concurrence, and no time perhaps more convenient for their meeting the attention and approbation of the States than the present, when they are generally convinced of the want of full powers, and are disposed to grant them. Any defects that have occurred to you, and no doubt many have from your situation and long service, you will oblige me in pointing out when you have leisure to write a few lines on the subject. It is of importance to make the articles of our union as complete as may be, and adequate to the great objects of the Confederacy, or
we

we shall suffer from internal divisions and foreign machinations.

I am happy to find a strong reinforcement is going south. If Arnold does not escape before their arrival, that abandoned man will probably meet the fate he deserves. The British affairs to the southward are now in a critical situation, and if we improve the advantages the conjunction opens to us, all will soon be restored there to the power of the States, Charles Town excepted, and even that, if our ally can succour us by water, I have my hopes may be recovered. These are my conjectures; how practicable or well founded, you are the best judge.

The officers to the other departments are not yet chosen.

JONES TO MADISON.

FREDERICKSBURG, 3ᵈ April, 1781.

DEAR SIR,

I arrived here the 7ᵗʰ day after my departure from Philadelphia. The sanguine hopes entertained before I set out of taking Arnold and his party at Portsmouth lessened as I advanced and at length were entirely lost by certain information that the British fleet were in the Bay after engaging that of the French off the Capes. The issue of the conflict has been variously reported—the account which obtains most credit is that the French disabled one of the British 74's but as the fleet left the bay in two days after she entered it in quest as it is said of the French fleet the presumption is they were not much injured. A report prevails that a second engagement took place the 24ᵗʰ near the Capes as a heavy a heavy cannonade was then heard in that quarter — of this as well as the first engagement it is probable you are better informed than we are as I met two expresses with despatches for Congress and Govr. Lee giving an account it was said of the above transaction and of the battle between Generals Greene and Cornwallis. I bespoke a pair of leather breeches of a breeches maker whose name I have forgot but who lives on the right hand side of Market street as you go to the market and the corner of 4th street, they are for Col. Taliferro and the price 600 dols. Be pleased to get them and deliver to the late General Woodford's servant, Daniel, when he calls for them.

Mrs. Woodford, as well as myself, will thank you for information when she is to apply for payment of the allowance made the widows of deceased officers, what the allowance is, and at what periods payable.

Since writing the above I have your letter by the post and find my conjectures true, that you knew more of the above transactions than we did. A letter from Weedon informs that 23 transports with troops commanded by Gen'l Phillips arrived Sunday week (the 25th ult.) at Lynhaven Bay, convoyed by the Chatham, Roebuck, Rainbow, the Hancock and 4 other frigates. Weedon further writes that a letter from Greene of the 23^d ult. mentions that his army is in high spirits and ready for another action, the enemy retreating and his army advancing. They left our wounded and 70 of their own.

JONES TO WASHINGTON.

PHILA: 16th May, 1781.

DEAR SIR,

Having returned to Congress a few days only, and private matters requiring my attention for great part of the time, I have not been able regularly to attend to business, or to acknowledge the receipt of your favour transmitted to Philadelphia after leaving it and sent after me to Virginia by Mr. Madison. The moment for successful operations against our enemies was certainly immediately after the disaster in Gardner's Bay, when, had it been embraced, the post at Portsmouth and the troops under Arnold, as well as the British ships then in Virginia must have fallen an easy conquest to our united efforts. For which purpose the State was, I believe, in readiness. Abortive as the project has proven, we yet hope for the best and that while it may be in the power of our ally to give us effectual aid in Chesapeake, and believe me, at no time was it more necessary than at present when all the lower country of our State from its great navigable waters are exposed to the ravage and rapine not only of British ships of war but of the vessels employed by the Board of Refugee Commissioners in New York. To you it is unnecessary to describe the distress of the inhabitants upon the navigable waters of Virginia. Your knowledge of the country enables you sufficiently to judge of it exclusive of such information as I doubt not you receive from that quarter. Had we a sufficient stock of arms distressing as it is to our militia to be so generally out on duty as it must be to them at this season of the year, I think they would do much in opposition to the enemy, supported even by no considerable body of regulars.

lars. But wanting arms, their negroes flying from them, and their prospects of making little or nothing from their estates to support their families and bear the burdens of the war, may shake their fidelity and attachment to the cause so far as to slacken their exertions if some succor is not afforded them by water to restrain the ravage of these plunderers. I mention these things as facts falling under my own observations before I left the State, that if they have not been more particularly communicated by others you might have some intimation of them.

The late movements of Cornwallis and Philips indicate a junction of their armies on the Roanoke from whence they may direct their operations north or south as they shall see best, without the fear of successful opposition, or may, it would seem cut off all communication between Virginia and the other southern States and reduce Gen'l Greene to the greatest extremity. From these dangers that at present threaten us a naval force sent to the Chesapeake would at once relieve us and admit Virginia to afford that succour to the other southern States they so much need. The great object of the enemy is undoubtedly the southern States, and it is submitted to your reflection how far you can support them by your influence in the destination of such aids as may arrive from Europe or the operation of that force now here. We are told all the ships of war have left New York with about 2,000 troops, after having once put back. Adieu. Pardon the haste of this letter which is written in Congress in consequence of the President's information our express was going off for Head Quarters.

JONES TO WASHINGTON.

PHILA: 31 May 1781

My DEAR SIR,

I am this moment informed that Mr. Rutledge is going to Head Quarters and have stolen out of Congress to give you a few lines to impress on you the necessity of taking some immediate steps for the succour of the southern department. The Marquis' letter will inform you of his situation and will of itself, without being enforced by me, shew the distress that must soon fall upon our State if not speedily succoured. For some days I have waited with impatience to hear from you, not doubting your anxiety for the southern States had determined you to measures for their support as far as you have the means in your power. This expectation and an opinion entertained that you must be fully informed of the late intelligence from Europe, have delayed my writing to mention these matters. The proposed mediation of the Imperial courts cannot be declined by the belligerent Powers, although delayed by France and Spain for a short time, to know the dispositions of the States. The most powerful exertions are necessary not only to give weight to the negociations of our plenipotentiary, but to recover our lost territory to prevent the difficulties of the proposition of *uti possidetis*. Congress are giving the necessary communications to the States and are endeavoring to stimulate them to emulation at this conjuncture, which more than ever calls for our own exertions in consequence of our disappointment from France. The aid in money though will, it is to be hoped, enable us to do something   what it would otherwise be in our power to effect. Virginia receiving so little aid from the

north

north occasions many of her citizens in their letters to the
delegates to insinuate that as they are not   and
safety, they care not for the southern States,   This notion
is but too prevalent and is of dangerous tendency to slacken
the   of the people and more readily dispose them
to submission.   I hope your deliberations with C^t. Rochambeau have determined upon relinquishing the idea of a certain conquest for the present and shew yourself in Virginia,
where I think your name and presence would be of infinite
service.   But, my dear Sir, I mention these things with the
utmost deference to your own judgment and feelings which
I am sure are equally touched with my own for the distress
of numbers in Virginia and as prompt to relieve them as
any person on earth, and I am satisfied will do so for us in
your power consistent with the general welfare.

We have before us a proposition for sending on an aid of
militia from this State and Maryland, but of all assistances
these are the worst and would avoid them if there was a
prospect of more effectual support.   Supplies of arms are
gone on and getting ready to go on, but these have been
greatly delayed for want of money.   .   .   .*

JONES TO JEFFERSON.

SPRING HILL, 16th April, 1781.

DEAR SIR,

The alliance of the American States being now completed
by the assent of the State of Maryland to the Articles of
Confederation, the future proceedings of Congress must be

*The ink of this letter has so faded as to be almost undecipherable.

governed

governed by those rules, and every deviation from them become matter of complaint or jealousy to the States. It would be wise, therefore, where defects appear to have them supplied in time, and while the temper of the States from recent experience of the want of competent powers in Congress for the purposes of war disposes them to do so. It appears to me indispensably necessary for the general welfare in time of war that Congress should be vested with a controlling power over the States sufficient to compel obedience to requisitions for men and money apportioned agreeable to the rules laid down. Without a coercive power for these purposes clearly vested in that body all future wars, as the present has done, must languish for want of proper authority to call forth the resources of the States. These aids should be as regularly and fully furnished by those States at ease and removed from danger as by those attacked and immediately exposed to it. Yet we have found these only when necessity and self preservation impelled them to exertions rendering those supplies the interest and safety of the whole required. And while some have strained every nerve and exhausted almost their whole strength in the struggle, others have been negligent and remiss in furnishing the proportions assigned. These delinquencies occasion discontents, prolong the war and expose the willing and obedient States to hardships, when justice requires that all contribute their property. How can this be effected without a controlling power in Congress for the purpose, I know not. Yet I know that without it we shall be a rope of sand, and the union be dissolved. It was made a question in Congress before I came away; I expect it will not be determined before I return, whether the United States in Congress

gress assembled had such a power; if not, whether it was not necessary they should have it. As the States have yielded to that body the right of making requisitions, does it follow Congress have the power by implication of enforcing obedience? If they now have this power, or not having it, the States should grant it them, how should the disobedient be punished? By shutting the ports, by a body of armed men, by deprivation of privileges or by what other method? These are nice and tender points to handle, but are unavoidable in the discussion of this question. How far it would be prudent to open them to the States, I know not. Could the business be effected without coming from Congress, by a voluntary declaration of the respective States of their sentiment upon the right of Congress to exercise such a power, it would, I think, be better; for I suspect such a recommendation coming from Congress would excite fears in the States, that there was a disposition in Congress to grasp dangerous powers. It is certainly a transcendent power, never to be used but in cases of absolute necessity and extremity. The acknowledgment, however, of such a power in Congress, might possibly supercede the use of it, as it would prove a weight impelling the States to action. If the States are ever to possess a formidable navy, which may be serviceable to them in time of war, the power of laying embargoes during war at least, should be vested in Congress. This appears necessary on many other accounts which cannot be unknown to you, and I confess myself at a loss to conjecture the reason of its omission in the articles.

If we are to have our great departments under the superintendence of ministers accountable for their conduct (and which was agreed upon and some of them chosen when I left

Congress

Congress, but which from a late letter from Madison will at length, I fear, be lost), it may be necessary, if any offences they may commit in the execution of their offices shall be punished in any of the courts now in being. As these officers will act throughout the States and can be resident in one only, there will be a difficulty in bringing them to trial and condign punishment without some special mode prescribed for the purpose. In this business, however, a great question arises. Can Congress, in other than military and maritime laws subject any citizen to death or other punishment than the laws of the State he belongs to inflict for such offenses? I have given your excellency much trouble in this letter. My apology is that I desire the sentiments of gentlemen of respectable abilities belonging to the State I represent in all very interesting questions, to assist my own judgment and opinion; and unless you forbid it I shall take the same liberty on future occasions when they present themselves.

I set out this day week for Philadelphia.

JONES TO WASHINGTON.

PHILA: 20 June 1781.

DEAR SIR,

I have your favour of the 7th inst. which gives me entire satisfaction of the propriety of your remaining with the Northern army and that it was out of your power from the small army under your command to afford any present succour to the southern States. The same sentiment I find was entertained by Governor Jefferson, to whom I presume you

you have written on the subject, but from the contents of a letter I have just received (or rather the delegates of Virginia) from R. H. Lee, inclosing one to be forwarded to you I expect you will be further solicited on that head, and as it may not be practicable for you speedily to give that gentleman an answer by conveyance from the present situation of the country, I shall as soon as an opportunity offers write to him upon the subject. From all the accounts we receive our greatest disadvantage lies in the greatest superiority of the enemy's horse, which being increased since their advancing into the country from the number of fine horses that have fallen into their hands to 7 or 800, so range about the country as to dismay the people not a little and keep them in continued alarm for the safety of their families. The superiority of the infantry I believe consists more in the distinction between regulars and militia than in numbers. This disadvantage in the cavalry cannot be surmounted by the State for want of equipments, of which they are very destitute. If they had them, the powers given by the Assembly to the Marquis to seize what horses may be necessary, would soon put him in condition to check their ravages; but at present and until these equipments can be furnished the country must be greatly exposed. Cannot you therefore spare Sheldon's horse for this service, and also Vanheer's corps? Every assistance in cavalry is essential, and these may I presume be soon with the Marquis. If you think the last mentioned horse to be trusted on the service, you will recollect that a part of them are now at Head Quarters, or at least I am so informed. The French cavalry, I take for granted from what you say, must remain with you; otherwise these being well mounted and equipped

6 *

equipped would be of more service than any other assistance you could immediately afford.   I wish you to consider
this matter of the cavalry, and give such orders as you shall
find convenient.   I have a letter by express from Col. Harrison, dated the 8th at Staunton, to which place the Assembly
adjourned after their dispersion and escape from Charlottesville.   He writes:

> Before this reaches you I dare say you will have heard how narrowly
> the whole Assembly escaped being made prisoners by Tarleton at Char-
> lottesville.   They had not left the town an hour before he entered at the
> head of 450 horse and mounted infantry.   Some stores are fallen into
> their hands, with three delegates and several other gentlemen.   Amongst
> them Mr. Lyons, Mr. Kinlock, Robert and William Nelson.   They are
> all paroled except Kinlock, and him they carried off.   Had it not been
> for the extraordinary exertions and kindness of a young gentleman who
> discovered their intentions and got round them in the night, not one man
> of those in town would have escaped; as it was, so incredulous were
> some of us, that it was with much difficulty they could be prevailed on
> to adjourn.
>
> We are in a most distressed condition from the sea to the mountains;
> so many fine horses have fallen into the hands of the enemy that they
> roam at large over all that country, and the Marquis is by no means able
> to check their progress.   He has power given him by the Assembly to
> impress horses wherever he can find them, but he has not necessaries to
> mount the men when he gets them.   This being the case, we know not
> what course to take to preserve the country from their ravages.   We want
> arms greatly for infantry, but when we have them it is difficult to find
> men to use them, owing to the danger their families are in from the horse.
> We have 600 fine men under Baron Steuben, which he will not carry
> into action.   What are his reasons I know not, but I can assure you his
> conduct gives universal disgust and injures the service much, the people
> complaining, and with reason, that they are dragged from their families
> at a time when they are most wanted to make bread for them, whilst the
> soldiers they have hired at a very great expence, lay idle.   In short, my
> dear sir, his conduct does great mischief, and will do more if he is not
>   recalled,

recalled, and I think it behooves you to bring it about. I assure you it is the wish and desire of every man that this event should take place. I believe him a good officer on the parade, but the worst in every other respect in the American army. I like the Marquis much and so does everybody in the country, but is he not too young for such a command as he has, and of such great consequence to the American cause, and this great country? Would not St. Clair, think you, from his experience, be useful here?

We have now no Executive in the State. For want of a Senate the governor will act no more, and the remainder of the council will not get together. I hope we shall set these matters right next week.

A copy of a letter from the Marquis of the 3^{d} inst. to Genl. Greene, intimates that he was ignorant till lately that Genl. Greene had ordered these levies to act in Virginia; but it does not appear he had orders from Genl. Greene upon the subject, as he complains in the letter that he had not heard from him for some time. Perhaps your interposition may be necessary upon this business to prevent misunderstanding. How far Col. H.'s opinion about the Baron requires your interference you will judge. I had heard some complaints of that gentleman before I left the State, but attributed them to his being long in the military line, unacquainted with the civil institution, and disgusted that his requisitions were not immediately complied with, rather than any other *quality*. However, if he has disgusted the people, prudence requires he should not be detached, but subject to the control of some superior officer, or recalled. These matters you will direct as you shall see fit for the service. Could not Genl. Greene be well spared from the south to take the command in Virginia? The great scene of action is there, and as you cannot be present, his abilities and experience may be very useful. Excuse the haste of this letter which I have been obliged to write in Congress.

JONES TO WASHINGTON.

PHILA. 3 July 1781.

DEAR SIR,

Such has been the situation of Virginia for some time past we have but little, and that very imperfect, intelligence of the transactions there. This may have been the case with you, and yesterday's post being the only one for some weeks that brought us letters. I enclose one received from Col. Carey for your perusal, knowing that your acquaintance with that gentleman will readily account for his prolixity and some inaccuracies.

Col. Temple, who arrived here a few days ago to forward [*] Dragoons, and which he expected to meet on the road, shewed me a letter dated the 21st ult. from the Marquis, pressing him to use all possible dispatch to join him with that corps of horse; that the enemy had left Richmond and were [*] down for Williamsburg. It is many weeks since this state was requested to equip this cavalry and send them to the Marquis's army, and we have been amused week after week that at least sixty of them were ready to march, and some times told they were marched; but such has been the supineness of this Assembly, they are not yet equipped and must be sent to Virginia to be mounted, if money can be procured to pay them part of what is due them for back pay. The militia called for, to go to the southward, will not be raised, and difficulties have been started to the 300 *particular militia* you requested; but I am in hopes they will be furnished. I will pardon all this if they fill up their Continental line, which they say is their design. In the

---

* Defaced by seal.

meantime

meantime they escape sending militia either south or north, unless the 300 you asked for are supplied. Our affairs have taken a most favorable turn to the south, and I hope the spirit of the people in that quarter is now so much roused that they will not be again reduced to the distressed state they were lately in. Their present resentment is high, and though partly ravaged, the country yet abounds with resources which when properly applied will make them formidable. Could the enemy but get a check by water in Virginia, in that state every thing would soon be restored and their violence as much humbled as lately it has been insulting.

When you have perused Col. Carey's history you may commit it to the flames.

JONES TO WASHINGTON.

PHILA: 6 August, 1781.

DEAR SIR,

I have received your favour of the 2^d inst. with the enclosures, and shall take proper care of them.

Mr. Morris setting out for Head Quarters in the morning, I embrace the opportunity to acknowledge the receipt of yours of the 10th ult., and to thank you for the copies of the intercepted letters. The originals were transmitted us by Dr. Franklin. These shew the continued delusion and folly of the British ministry, now rendered more conspicuous by our late successes.

From Carolina by the last flag which left Charles Town on Thursday last week, we learn that the enemy had abandoned 96 and indeed all their posts were evacuated but Charles Town,

Town, where the troops were near all arrived; the last detachment from Ireland reduced about half by the march to relieve 96; Lord Rawdon in Charles Town, much indisposed but bound soon for England; and that Leslie was met by the flag on board Carrisfoot (?) going to Charles Town to take the command. A packet was just arrived from England, by which accounts were received that the greatest part of the fleet with the Statia plunder had been taken by Admiral la M. Picquet, and carried into France — very pleasing news if it prove true.

No late accounts from Europe or the W. Indies. The Dons seem to play the game wholly for themselves, instance their avidity for territorial cession on the Mississippi and the exclusive navigation of that river, and the late extraordinary capitulation at Pensacola. The neutral combination has at length drawn from Britain an instruction to her ships of war and armed vessels not to interrupt the commerce of the Baltic. We are told Holland is disposed to an alliance with these States; it may be so, but I fear she has a remnant of Spanish indolence and inactivity that requires beating before she will rouse to vigorous action, for as yet I discover but feeble efforts. Let us look at home where matters are more pleasing from the successes of the present campaign, and if we pursue our advantage [it] will place us in a respectable situation before the negotiators at the Congrèss when they convene. And if you shall be able to push the point at New York and be ultimately crowned with success, I shall be very indifferent about Spanish or Dutch alliances, especially the first; as I confess I do not relish their behaviour to us on more occasions than one. But enough of this.

We

We have had much debate about Vermont; nothing yet determined, but *think* it will terminate in appointing persons to settle with them the terms of their admission into the union.

By the Marquis you will be informed of the British fleet moving up the bay the 31st ult. with about 3000 troops on board destined it was supposed for Baltimore. They had been embarked some days, and in the road, waiting I presume for intelligence. Perhaps the interception of the southern mail afforded them what they wanted, though it is said a vessel came in from New York. Gov.r Lee's letter is the 4th and the fleet not then in sight of Annapolis, which makes me suspect they must have been detained by contrary winds, or put into Potomack. We shall, if they are come up the Bay, hear more to morrow. If we do before Mr. Morris sets off, you shall have the information.

Mrs. Washington was out at Col. Bland's when your letter arrived. I have sent her letter by one of her servants.

JONES TO MADISON.

SPRING HILL, 21st May, 1782.

DEAR SIR,

The friendly visits of my neighbours and acquaintances since my return have been and still continue to occupy my time, having not been free from company since the day after my getting home. Of course I have thought little of those matters which used, while in Philadelphia, to employ our attention, and have not yet fixed the time of my visit to Richmond, which will be regulated by information from there. Our last accounts (whether true I know not) but

your

your advices by the post will inform you, say there was a House on Wednesday last; if so, I shall in eight or ten days pay my respects to them. It is said several petitions will be presented urging a further emission of paper currency as indispensably necessary to supply the scarcity of specie. Some through folly, others from wicked acts may countenance this measure, but I cannot believe there can be found in the Assembly a majority of those characters until the fatal adoption of the proposition shall convince me of my mistake. It is certain that specie is either very scarce, or, if in the country, locked up, as the want of it is universally complained of by the planter and merchant. It must be very scarce, or our commerce very languid, as I am told good merchantable flour may be purchased over the mountains for 7s.6d. p^r hundred, and I know tobacco (upland too) will not produce upon this river 2d. cash. The reason assigned [is] want of money to purchase. Imported articles in general 100 per cent. higher than in Philadelphia, and as great part of the goods for sale come from that quarter and of late from N. York, *then* it is easy to account for the drain of specie, and what must be the consequence to these States from such a ruinous traffic and a hampered commerce.

I have not been able to find your pamphlet among my books and papers. Should I come across it, you may be certain proper care shall be taken of it, and conveyed by the first safe hand. Did you not lend it to Mr. Lee or Col. Bland? I think you had it from me sometime I came away, and for the perusal of one of those gentlemen. Pray, my friend, let me have the Revolutionist from No. 4. I have it to that number. The April packet from England may be daily expected at New York. By her we may probably
hear

hear the result of the proceedings in consequence of Genl. Conway's motion.* I hear little of recruiting our line. The business, they say, is at a stand for want of money, as indeed is almost every other public exertion. Some military men say they could recruit our line if they had a specie bounty to offer. This cannot be furnished until the taxes bring it in, and then, if at all, will not be productive until October. Virginia will, therefore, this summer have few men in the field, unless for the spur of the occasion. Perhaps the Assembly may think it necessary to order out a body for the [†].

Mrs. Jones begs her compliments to the ladies and joins me in the same to Col. Bland and yourself.‡

On 25th February Conway had made a motion in the House of Commons against continuing the war against the States. It was defeated by a majority of one vote. Five days later an address to the King of the same purport passed the House by a majority of nineteen.

---

*On the 25th February Conway had made a motion in the House of Commons against continuing the war against the States. It was defeated by a majority of one vote. Five days later an address to the King of the same purport passed the House by a majority of nineteen.

† Torn by seal.

‡ "At present all my colleagues have left Congress except Col. Bland, and it is a crisis which calls for a full representation from every State."—*Madison to Madison*, May 20, 1782.

JONES TO MADISON.

SPRING HILL, 25 June 1782

DEAR SIR,

Your favour of the 4th instant, and the packet of newspapers by Mr. Webb, went to Richmond and were returned to Fredericksburg, where I received them the last week; but no letter from you that post. From Richmond I had written you a long letter, and, getting home in time for the post at Fredericksburg, added a short one of some other matters that occurred after my getting home. These letters, I am told last night, have been intercepted near Onion's works in Maryland, and conveyed (probably) to Sir Guy Carleton before this; and you will I expect have an opportunity of reading them in the royal Gazette soon, to which I must refer you for their contents, having no copy and not well recollecting the whole. I fear there are some observations I could wish not to be public. If any such, they must relate to some transactions of the Assembly or individual members, but I think none of them very reprehensible, though known to the parties. I was particular respecting the petition you mentioned to have been communicated to the minister, and this may induce a publication. I mentioned the continuation of the old delegates by a vote, but which I afterwards found to be a mistake, the vote being postponed until the bill had passed repealing the law that rendered yourself and J. J. ineligible. The allowance 8 dollars per day; no directions given for the settlement of the time past, although the sense of the House asked by the auditors respecting the daily allowance. Jefferson, Mason, Randolph, Lee and Walker, have been appointed to state

the

the title of Virginia to western territory — Committee to draw instructions for delegates respecting western territory.

C. Boneouski [?] had not reached Richmond when I left it. [I] hear since he was there, but not likely to succeed. This day's post will I expect communicate the result of his application.

In the intercepted letter I transmitted you a bill of Mr. Ross's in Whitesides in my favor for two hundred and some dollars, to pay M. C. Griffin, or if he was not in immediate want, a Messrs. Butler & Co., which Mr. Solomon could inform you of. I that week received a line from my friend Griffin requesting a remittance of the money. I have wrote to day to Mr. Ross to renew the draft and forward it to me, and it shall go forward as soon as I receive it. Pray present my compliments to Mr. Griffin and acquaint him with the circumstance. I have not yet concluded on my return to Philadelphia, but think I shall do it at least for the fall, if I can prevail upon Mrs. Jones to accompany me with Joe. She is now up in Orange on a visit to her father. If I visit Philadelphia, it will be about the middle or twentieth next month. You will therefore be so obliging as to inquire about a lodging furnished, with two lodging rooms, servant's room, and two entertaining rooms and the use of the kitchen; or a convenient house furnished, that if I come up you may be able to engage me one upon as moderate terms as you can. As soon as I make up my mind upon the journey, you shall be informed. Mr. Lee has I expect joined you, as he was to set out in a few days after me leaving him in Richmond. Pray make my compliments to Col. Bland, and Mr. Lee, if present.

JONES TO MADISON.

FREDERICKSBURG, 1st July 1782.

DEAR SIR,

I have no letter from you by this post. Expecting to receive from Mr. Ross a duplicate of the bill which fell into the hands of the robbers and forward it to you this week, I came to town to-day, but have no letter from him. Col. Monroe writes me he promised to send it. My friend Griffin will, therefore, be obliged to wait longer than I intended and hoped he would. Mr. Ross was also to have sent me a further draft on Philadelphia for my present supply if I went forward, which it was my intention to do about the middle of this month or the 20th at further.

Be kind enough to have the inclosed advertisement inserted twice or thrice in the Packet, and inform Mr. Solomon of it; that in case Cyrus is apprehended he may receive him and have him confined until I come up or give directions about him. He was seen in the city since my departure.

I must refer you to our friend Randolph for the news of Richmond, who is on the spot and can give it you truly. We have a report here that a large fleet had passed the capes, steering eastward, and it is said to be French; but the story is so vague I regard it not. Mr. Henry and Col. Lee have left the Assembly, which is still sitting. Something has been done for recruiting the army, but what, I cannot certainly inform you. It is expected it will bring men into the field. We heard great complaints before I left Philadelphia of the scarcity of money in this State. They were well founded and increase every day. If there
is not

is not a real scarcity, those who possess the money lock it up, which produces all the inconveniences of a scarcity. Should I pay you a visit, I shall find it difficult to procure cash sufficient for my expenses.

JONES TO MADISON.

SPRING HILL, 8th July 1782

DEAR SIR,

I intended when I left Richmond to set out for Philadelphia about the middle of this month, but from a manœuvre of Mr. Ross's in settling the balance due from Mr. Braxton, and which had by the Executive been ordered to me, I am disappointed of the means necessary for the journey and am left to my own resources, which I am determined shall not be applied to [the] public any further than is unavoidable — I mean in the line of my appointment to Congress. When I shall be properly furnished and I see a prospect of continued supply, I may perhaps revisit Philadelphia. At present it depends on Mr. Ross, who instead of furnishing me money or bills as promised has settled Mr. Braxton's balance of about £200 by transmitting mè your order on me given to Whiteside for the money I procured before I left Philadelphia, and which the Governor and also your letter informed was paid. This order I expect was taken by Mr. Whiteside as a voucher to transmit to Mr. Ross. The disappointment, however, considering the violent heat of the weather, proves agreeable on that account, though I could have wished to have gone northward before the commencement of the sickly season. I have
never

never heard from Mr. Solomon* whether the wagonners delivered him the tobacco they carried from here.

The French army are on their march. The Legion came over to Falmouth yesterday, and the infantry are expected to be there next Thursday. Ct. Rochambeau on his way, quartered at old Mr. Hunter's the night before last. Mrs. Bland was a few days past at Col. Dangerford, on her way to Philadelphia. She intended Dr. Lee should have escorted her, but the Dr. missing her letter occasioned a disappointment. When I saw her she was in doubt when she should proceed and by whom be attended.

One of the ships sent for the tobacco I am told has been seized and will be proceeded against in the admiralty court—the cause, having on board a quantity of goods which was sold or offered for sale to some of the inhabitants. I believe they came well provided for such a traffic, but this step will probably suspend all further commercial intercourse.

If Mr. Ross puts me in a situation to proceed you shall be informed. In the meantime you will not omit your inquiries about a lodging should I have occasion for one. We have had a great drought, and the hottest weather for the time of the year I ever experienced. Our crops of small grain [are] short and not so good as usual. Randolph I understand will be up in the fall.

---

* Hayne Solomon, described by Madison as a " Jew broker."

JONES TO MADISON.

FREDERICKSBURG, 16th July, 1782.

* * The French army have all passed Rappahannock at Falmouth. The last division will move to-morrow from that place. Their progress through this part of the country furnishes some of the inhabitants with cash to pay the taxes. About 500 convalescents remain at York. I expected Mr. Lee would have been with you some time past, but hear by Col. Monroe he only left Chantilly about ten days ago.

JONES TO MADISON.

SPRING HILL, 22^d July, 1782.

DEAR SIR,

The reason why Williamsburg and its neighbourhood were mentioned as the place supposed to be attended to be alluded to by the correspondent of a certain gentleman, proceeded from my mentioning to Mr. H-d-y what had been communicated, and his observing that he supposed it proceeded from a report that had been circulated of a petition set on foot in Williamsburg, praying the Legislature to accept any reasonable terms that should be offered, but which had been suppressed upon Ct. Ro-h-b-u's sending of his aids to remonstrate to the parties on the imprudence of the measure, which suspended all further proceedings in the matter. This Mr. H. mentioned as a report he had heard, but doubted its truth. I asked some other gentlemen if they had heard any thing of it, and wished to know if there was any foundation for the report, supposing what had been communicated must have proceeded from this report. I was the
more

more desirous to learn the truth, that, if it was a misrepresentation of the character of the people, these might not bear the aspersion. But my inquiries served only to convince me the report respecting the petition in Williamsburg was groundless; and I imagine the people there suspected the intelligence communicated might proceed from the above misrepresentation, and thinking themselves in some measure injured by the report, they took up the matter in the manner the paper I enclosed you exhibits. They supposed your communication to me was local, as I mentioned the matter as from you, but in general terms in the manner you stated; and it was the previous report only that fixed it on Williamsburg and its neighborhood was groundless, and my inquiries lead me to suspect no other part of the country as manifesting a disposition to precipitate matters.

We have some agreeable reports from our quarter since the last post. Your letters, which I expect by the post to-day, will I hope confirm them. The evacuation of Charles Town, a successful attack of the Dutch upon a British convoy in the Baltic, and the accession of the 7th state of the provinces to the treaty with the States of America. The first and last are probable, and have been expected; and I am not disposed to discredit the other, especially when I reflect on the bravery of the Dutch in the few conflicts they have had with the British since the commencement of hostilities.

* * Have you heard any thing of Cyrus? Should he be apprehended let him be confined in prison until I come up, unless an opportunity present itself of shipping him for the W. Indies, where if I recover him I mean he shall be transported and sold.

JONES TO WASHINGTON.

PHILADA, 27th February, 1783.

DEAR SIR,

Your favors of the 14th December last and the 11th inst. have been duly received. A series of ill-health through the fall and the greatest part of the winter, and which until very lately rendered my attendance in Congress seldom and very irregular, must be my apology for suffering the first to remain so long unanswered.

Congress have been for some time past almost wholly employed in devising some general and adequate funds for paying the interest and, in time, sinking the principal, of the public debt, as well as to provide for future loans, should the continuance of the war render borrowing necessary. Difficulties, apparently insurmountable, presented themselves in almost every stage of the business, owing to the different circumstances of the several States, and the necessity that the subjects selected for taxation to form the funds should operate throughout them all, generally and equally, or nearly so, to make them acceptable. After opening and discussing a variety of questions, no object has been yet discovered, to which so few objections lie, as the impost duty formerly recommended to the States, and which, with some alterations from the former plan to obviate the objections that have been raised, has been agreed to in a Committee of the Whole, and will I think be finally adopted. What this duty when granted by the States will amount to annually is very uncertain. In time of peace there can be no doubt but it will be considerable, and for years prove an increasing fund; but it is thought by no means adequate to the payment of the interest and sinking the

7 *

the principal of the public debt. Other means have, therefore, been considered in aid of the impost duty — land,
polls, salt, wine, spirits, tea, &c. These last being what
are called luxuries it is thought may bear a small tax in
addition to the impost duty. I fear at present that few of
these will go down, and that we shall be obliged at last to
rest the payment of the public debt upon the mode prescribed by the Confederation — (requisitions, proportioned
on the States according to the value of land, buildings,
&c. — a plan for obtaining which scale of proportion has
been digested and agreed upon in Congress, and will immediately go on to the States,) and the produce of the 5 per
cent. duty, if granted. A small poll tax, did not the Constitution of Maryland stand in the way, might probably
succeed, as it would operate more equally perhaps than
any other, and may be adopted, allowing Maryland to
substitute some other adequate and productive fund in its
room. A short time will bring to a conclusion our efforts
on this business, which I am in hopes will terminate in the
adoption of such measures as may be acceptable to the
States, and produce the granting such funds as will restore
public credit, give value to the great mass of depreciated
certificates, and enable Congress to render to every class
of the public creditors ample justice. Congress have the
purest intentions towards the public creditors, and will use
their best exertions in obtaining from the States the means
to do them speedy and complete justice. Such is their
opinion of the merit and services of the army, that did it
not wound the sense of justice, they want not the inclination to give them the preference to any other class of creditors. But equity and sound policy forbid discriminations.
One

One ground of discontent in the army, and on which they found the opinion that justice is not intended to be done to them, is the delay in complying with their requests. But with those acquainted with the deliberations of public bodies, and especially if so mixed a body as that of Congress, allowances will be made for slow determination. Every class of public creditors must know the inability of Congress to pay their demands, unless furnished with the means by the several States, and the exertions of that body have not been wanting heretofore to obtain the means, though they have not produced the desired effect. The measures now digesting will, there is good reason to expect, prove more efficacious for obvious reasons.

Reports are freely circulated here that there are dangerous combinations in the army, and within a few days past it has been said that they are about to declare that they will not disband until their demands are complied with. I trust these reports are not well founded, and that the army will exercise awhile longer at least, that patient forbearance which hath hitherto so honourably distinguished them. To you it must be unnecessary to observe that when all confidence between the civil and military authority is lost, by intemperate conduct or an assumption of improper power, especially by the military body, the Rubicon is passed, and to retreat will be very difficult from the fears and jealousies that will unavoidably subsist between the two bodies. To avoid therefore the adoption by the army of any hasty and rash measure, should employ the attention and draw forth the exertions of every worthy officer in it; for from these alone can opposition be expected. The ambition of some, and the pressure of distress in others, may produce dangerous

ous combinations, founded on the pretence that justice is delayed, and will be refused to them. The pretext is plausible and ensnaring, and may draw into engagements the unsuspecting, honest soldier, from which it will be difficult to extricate himself, even when he sees the dangers they lead to. If there are men in the army who harbour wicked designs, and are determined to blow the coals of discord, they will gradually endeavour to hurt the reputation of those averse to their projects, and by sinister practices lessen their weight and influence among the soldiery. I have lately heard there are those who are abandoned enough to use these arts to lessen your popularity* in the army in hopes ultimately the weight of your opposition will prove no obstacle to their ambitious designs. If this be true, and they are likely to succeed I own it will prove a bad prognostic of the future and I shall be among the number of those who entertain fears of the army and doubt that peace will not be followed by its usual blessings to America. Whether to temporize, or oppose with steady unremitting firmness what is supposed to be in agitation of dangerous tendency, or that may be agitated, must be left to your own sense of propriety and better judgment.

With respect to the business of Vermont, I think you need not be uneasy from apprehensions that the army or any part of them employed to enforce a compliance with the act of the 5th of December last, should the people of Vermont refuse a compliance with that demand, at least for some time to come if ever. To go into detail upon this matter would be prolix and rather improper for the

* Washington has written over this the word "reputation."

scope

scope of a letter. It cannot be denied that the act of
Congress of the   of August opened the prospect to
Vermont of an acknowledgement of her independence and
admission into the union. Although it gave ground of
hope, it was not conclusive, and the legislature of Vermont
absolutely rejecting the offer, and recommending to the
people an inviolable adherence to their union and en-
croachments on the neighboring States, (and which, as
well as other unwarrantable acts they have unjustly concealed from the public in their remonstrance) released
Congress from their offer, and left them at liberty afterwards to accept or refuse as they saw fit, when Vermont,
repenting of her conduct at a future period, complied. A
particular state of things produced the act of Congress, a
change of circumstances afterwards dictated the delay in
determining on their proposition, and the report of a committee to whom it was referred. The report authorizes
observations I decline to make. This proceeding in Congress they stile a violation of the compact entered into
with them. There has always been a strong opposition to
the claims of Vermont and their admission into the union.
Virginia has generally been among the number of her opponents, not so much perhaps upon the question of independence, as the impolicy of her admission into the union
while several very important questions of local concern
remained undetermined; and until these great points are
settled, the consent of Virginia I expect will be withheld,
and if before obtained, it will be a sacrifice of her opinion
to the peace and common weal of the United States. If
Vermont confines herself to the limits assigned her, and
ceases to encroach upon and disturb the quiet of the ad-
joining

joining States, at the same time avoiding combinations or acts hostile to the U. States, she may be at rest within her limits, and by patient waiting the convenient time may ere long be admitted to the privileges of union. The influence Vermont has gained in the army and in some of the States that espouse her cause, do little credit to the parties concerned, and to this influence is in a great measure to be ascribed the variable, indecisive conduct of Congress respecting the claims of that people. The remonstrance states the receipt of *official* letters recommending a compliance with the act of Congress, and intimates yours to be of the number, and that these communications influenced them to comply. The assertion is wrong as to yours, and may be equally false as to others, and is one proof among a variety of others of the disingenuity and want of candour in Vermont. It exhibits also very little respect to this body, when they ascribe their compliance to other motives than the recommendation of Congress.

Seven States have voted 5 years' whole pay as the commutation for the half pay to the officers; but the resolution has not passed the House being postponed for the present from an opinion prevalent with many that the consent of nine States is necessary to give it validity. Delaware and Georgia are absent, were they represented probably the vote would be sufficient.

That we shall have peace soon is almost reduced to a certainty, but my fears are it will not be attended with those blessings generally expected. There are so many great questions very interesting to particular States unsettled, which require speedy determination to preserve quiet, that it is difficult to avoid uneasy impressions for their consequences

quences. The present conjunction perhaps, above all others America has experienced, calls for good dispositions in the States, and moderation and wisdom in their councils. May the spirit of union govern them.

JONES TO WASHINGTON.

PHILA: 6 May, 1783

DEAR SIR,

We have at length got through the plan of funds to be recommended to the States for their adoption. It has been the most difficult and perplexing discussion of any that has engaged the attention of this body for some time. The various objects to be combined and the different interests to be reconciled to make the system palatable to the States, were a work not easily or speedily to be effected; and although it was the wish of many to settle the plan upon clear and unquestioned principles of finance, yet such were the prejudices of some States and of some individuals, and such their jealousies, we were obliged to take a middle course with respect to its duration, and the appointment of collectors, or hazard ultimately the loss of the measure. As it stands I believe it will answer the purposes intended, if the States will grant their concurrence. A copy will be transmitted to you for your and the army's information.

As the state of our finances at present is such as to make it difficult for the officer now at the head of that department, much more so for any new hand who might succeed him to form the necessary arrangements for obtaining money sufficient for disbanding the army, Mr. Morris has agreed to act until that business is accomplished, and will

I hope

I hope be able to effect it to the satisfaction of the army. But from appearances the business of disbanding will be more distant than many at first apprehended, if that measure, as it seems to be proper it should, goes hand in hand with the evacuation of our country by the British forces. By this time you are better able to judge of the views and designs of Sir G. Carleton, or of those who direct his movements, as I presume the intended interview took place, though I confess I thought there was indelicacy in the manner of that gentleman's mentioning his proposed attendants. In every thing else, but that of evacuation (and they may be doing all they can in that for any thing I know) they seem to act with fairness and liberality; and I should be sorry to find them in that, or any other instance, practising the old game of deception. We have reports something of this sort appearing in their conduct respecting the negros in their possession claimed by our citizens. These relations come from men of character, and until the contrary is ascertained of what they assert, credit will be given to these reports. No proclamations can authorize a refusal of property to those who claim under the article of the treaty, and establish their right by satisfactory proof. Col. F. Thornton, of Machodack, about two years ago lost many of his negros who went on board some of the British ships of war up Potomack. He wrote to me the other day about them. These I believe are not sanctioned by proclamation, and yet I suspect if the old gentleman was to send a person to claim them, his labors would be lost. If what we are told respecting the conduct of those in power in N. York concerning the claimed property of the American citizens be true, it will prove an effectual bar to the

restoration

restoration of confiscated estates, had there been a disposition in the States before to render them. I wished to have seen the treaty faithfully executed on both sides, but where arts and prevarication take place on our side, they are apt to prevail on the other. I proceed immediately to Virginia in order to attend the Assembly now convening, and shall thank you for any information respecting these matters you can properly communicate, that the truth may be known and misrepresentations, if any prevail, removed. If anything occurs to you which you do not choose to communicate directly to the Executive with respect to the arrangements necessary to be made on a peace, and shall confide them to me, proper attention shall be paid to your observations.

———————

JONES TO MADISON.

RICHMOND, 25 May, 1783.

DEAR SIR,

After resting at home two days I set out for this place, where I arrived on Tuesday last, and took my seat in the House some days before my colleague, who made his appearance for the first time yesterday. My arrival was seasonable with respect to a bill then before the House for postponing the collection of the taxes for the ease of the people until December next, that, as it was said by Mr. H—y who supported the measure, they might enjoy a short respite from bearing the burthen of taxes—a kind of holiday to rejoice more cheerfully on the glorious termination of the war. This bill was by order to be considered that day in a committee of the whole, and I was in time to give such information to the committee as to induce them to come to

no

no conclusion *then*, but to rise and ask leave to sit again, that they might have an opportunity before they determined the question, to hear the contents of the proceedings relative to that subject which might be daily expected from Congress. A bill which was called by some an excellent bill, was also before the House and has since passed the delegates. Its object is the rendering members of Congress in future ineligible to the Legislature. I expect it will also obtain the assent of the Senate. You will be under no difficulty in discovering the policy of this bill. It was proposed in the Committee of the House to reduce the number to three, but the question was determined in the negative. The laws against the importation of British merchandise are repealed, and their vessels have been permitted to land their cargoes. A revision of the salaries of the officers of the government was under consideration of a committee yesterday. A small majority continued the 1000*l* p^r ann. to the governor; the privy councillors reduced to 2400*l*. The judges of the Court of Chancery could in the Committee be raised to only 400 each. Whether as much will be allowed the judges of the General Court and of the Admiralty show some doubt, especially the latter, as J—h J—hn—n and his adherents are for reductions. The plan of Congress for obtaining funds from the States was laid before the House and read the day before yesterday. This system appears to me at present to have more friends than enemies, and I think the former will increase, the latter diminish. I may however be mistaken in my conjecture, and the result of our deliberations on it may prove that I am so. For you are to learn how fickle and variable the conduct of this body has been in this business. As a further

ther proof of it, I will only mention that when I came here I found a bill had been ordered to re-enact the 5 p^r ct. Some, R. H. L. and his adherents, are opposed to the measure; others, are opposed in part, disliking the clause declaring the act irrevocable, and that the State is not to have credit for the surplus of tax beyond her quota of the annual demand, if there should be a surplus. These are a kind of neutrals on the whole, which each side hopes to gain. They express their wish to support the measure, but these objects repel them. The chief of these I have yet found out are J. T—yl—r and G—e N—l—s. These are also strong advocates for a revision of the scale for loan office certificates. For the measure, P. H—y, the Sp—k—r, and several other respectable members.

That part of the delegates' letter as respected the treaty of commerce with Great Britain, was referred to the Committee on Trade, with instructions to make a speedy report, which was done yesterday morning as an instruction to our delegates in Congress. It proposed only entering into a treaty upon liberal and generous principles, reserving a right to give bounties on tonnage, &c. The report not pleasing the House, a debate ensued, which terminated in a ⟨blank⟩ of it to a committee of the whole, into which the House immediately resolved. A large field was then opened and great commercial knowledge, or rather a want of it, displayed. Finding the business taking the turn it did, and likely to be delayed and at last, perhaps, produce instructions rather hurtful than useful, I took the liberty to recommend a short instruction to the purport of that you will receive. I did this from a knowledge that something similar was the object of Congress and the best that

at

at present and speedily could be given. A general concurrence ensued, the other motions withdrawn, and the one sent you passed immediately and unanimously.

The officers of our line and of Genl. Clark's regiment have presented memorials stating that they understand the lands on the Cumberland reserved for the officers have been great part of it (the best of the lands) taken up by others; that it was greatly short of the quantity necessary to answer the purpose, and requesting a district of country on the N. W^r of the Ohio to be assigned them. There appears a general disposition to gratify them. I could wish if anything is, or is meant to be done in Congress respecting our cession, we should be informed of it without delay.

Sir Guy Carleton's conduct respecting the negro property is considered by many here as a departure from the provisional articles, and will be made use of to justify a delay in paying the British debts.

The treasurer informs me a remittance to the delegates has been made since I came away of £1000; also of £200 to yourself on account of the balance due. Until an account is returned to him of the distribution of the sums remitted, our account cannot be closed. You will therefore attend to this. Pray make my compliment to the gentlemen of our delegation and the ladies of your family.

P. S. No letter from you this post. The notion of a convention seems for the present to be laid aside. My seal and letter for the president of the college are committed to the care of Mr. Wythe, who takes his departure for Williamsburg to-day, being the last of the chancery session.

JONES TO MADISON.

RICHMOND, 31 May, 1783.

DEAR SIR,

I should have been uneasy on account of your health had I not heard letters were received from you by the last post, as I had none myself this or the last week. If you wrote as I suppose you did, the letters must have either miscarried or been stopt at Fredericksburg. We have not yet been in a Committee on the papers from Congress, and I begin to fear the opposition will be more powerful than the last week I apprehended. Individual and local considerations appear to me to be too general and so fixed as to afford but small consolation to those who wish the policy of the State to be governed by more enlarged and liberal principles. I do not, however, yet despair of the Assembly's adopting the plan recommended by Congress for establishing funds to discharge the national debt; although a fact mentioned to me yesterday evening (that P. H. was deserting the measure) alarms my fears. Since my last, the bill for postponing to the 20th of November next the making distress for the taxes has passed the delegates by a majority of 13, and was the day before yesterday assented to by the Senate. Hurtful and dangerous as this step will I fear prove, it was warmly espoused by Mr. H—y, opposed by his antagonist, and every effort made to fix the day to an earlier period, but in vain. It is true the people are in many places distressed for Indian corn. Tobacco, flour and hemp have greatly increased in their price, while imported articles have considerably decreased. Yet such was the rage for giving ease to the people, nothing could be offered sufficiently forcible to prevent the suspension taking place.

The

The memorial of the officers of the Virginia line has been reported by the committee reasonable, and the several resolutions reported by the committee in consequence stand referred to the Committee of the Whole on the state of the Commonwealth. This proceeding is repugnant to the cession of the lands beyond the Ohio, and giving a preference to the officers of our line to those of other States, will excite discontents in the Army, as well as involve us in controversy with Congress. These obstacles, if they shall not ultimately defeat, will at least delay our determination. Whatever is meant to be done respecting the cession should be hastened, and the result communicated as soon as possible.

A voluminous tobacco bill has taken up great part of this week. We got rid of it yesterday, and have sent it to the Senate. A bill to repeal an act of the last session "to prevent intercourse with and the admission of British subjects into this State," and another bill in consequence to repeal the law declaring who shall be deemed citizens, are before the House. The two great leaders of the House are upon these bills united, both concurring in the repeal of the former and opposing the passage of the latter, but I think upon different principles. The one, P. H., conceiving it the true interest of the State to admit all classes of persons without distinction; of the other, not only perhaps for the same reason, but for others also, and in particular, that he thinks the articles of the treaty preclude us from discrimination. The citizen bill may come under consideration to day. The advocates for it are disposed to exclude all natives who have left the country since April '75, all who, having taken the oath of allegiance to the States or held offices under either

from

from that period, have gone over to the enemy. These matters are premature and I could have wished them to have been delayed to a future day. They may probably be yet postponed.

Sir Guy Carleton's conduct respecting the negros is considered here as evasive of the article of the treaty, and confirms in their opinions, if it does not increase the number opposed to the payment of British debts. Time for payment and deduction of the interest during the war, seem to be generally the sentiment, and to be desired by many of these who are supposed to be most attached to the British interest.

The day before yesterday we were informed that about 100 of Baylor's regiment of cavalry were on their way in North Carolina to this State, without any officer above subalterns to command them. The reasons assigned by them for their conduct [are] want of provision for themselves and horses. I suspect the true ground of their desertion to be the order for their remaining when the infantry were to march to this State, which I think took place before I left Philadelphia. That they might not disturb the inhabitants in their route by plunder and probably occasion the shedding of blood in consequence, General Morgan, who was here with some other officers, was sent to take the command of them and conduct them to Winchester.

Pray inform me what has been done respecting the Indians since I left Congress. Whether any steps have been taken in consequence of the orders given the Commander in chief concerning them. Tell Mr. Mercer I must leave him for the present to his friend Monroe and other correspondents.

The

The bill rendering delegates to Congress ineligible in future to the legislature has passed the Senate. Do you come in and when?

JONES TO MADISON.

RICHMOND, 8 June, 1783.

DEAR SIR,

I am still deprived of the pleasure of hearing from you, no letter having arrived by this post. Col. Taliaferro informs me he directed Smith to send forward any letters for me to Fredericksburg, where I suspect they are stopped. I shall write to Smith upon the subject by this post. Your letters will find me here till the last week, or at least the 25th of this month.

We have not yet taken up the plan of Congress for general revenue. It is agreed to do it next Monday or Tuesday. Mr. R. H. L. is opposed to it *in toto*. Mr. H—y I understand thinks we ought to have credit for the amount of the duty, under an apprehension we shall consume more than our proportion, or, in other words, that we shall by agreeing to the impost as recommended pay more than our quota of the debt. J. Taylor wholly against the plan. G. N—l—s thinks with H—y. The Speaker is for it. B—x—n, I am told is so too, but he has not said as much to me. The two first named being in the opposition is what alarms me. Mr. H—y, I am told, was at first in favor of the impost and had early in the session concurred in bringing in a bill to revive the former law, but has since changed his opinion. The members seem to be very much divided. I wish we could hear whether any of the States have adopted it.

Yesterday

Yesterday our delegates to Congress were elected—Jefferson, Hardy, Mercer, Lee, Monroe. Mr. Griffin was voted for and had near fifty votes; but three objections were started against him which I am told had weight or were made so to keep him out: his seat in the Court of Appeals, his residence in Philadelphia, and just before the ballot was taken some whispers were spread he was withdrawn for the reasons above, which it is said lost him some votes. The two first mentioned reasons were the chief obstacles. One was publicly mentioned in the House, which gave me an opportunity of endeavoring at least to obviate the objection. My compliments to Mr. Mercer and inform him what he had heard of a report circulated to his prejudice either never existed or has died away so as not to be mentioned or even whispered. Mr. Short is elected to supply the vacancy in the Council.

In consequence of the memorial of the officers of the Virginia line a report from the Committee of Prop and G: to whom it was referred has been under consideration. It was proposed to allow our line the whole of their land on the n. side of the Ohio, with an additional quantity as a gratuity, on pretence that the Cumberland tract was greatly deficient in quantity and quality. Also to bear the expense of the location. This report was so repugnant to the cession to Congress and to the remonstrance in 1779, whereby the legislature promised to furnish lands beyond the Ohio to the States wanting lands for their lines, that I could not help opposing it, which has given it a check for the present, and upon consideration I am convinced a great majority will disapprove the report. Mr. H—y warmly espoused the report. R. H. L. when it was discussed [was] unable to attend

8 *

tend being somewhat indisposed. What side he may take on the next discussion of the report I cannot learn. Be it as it may, I think if they unite in this business, they cannot carry it. Congress having not accepted the cession, and declined to assign their reasons for delay, will produce *at least* a determination fixing the time when, if the cession is not accepted, it shall become void, if not an immediate re-vocation of it. I am not without hopes this business may yet be concluded so as to answer the views of Congress, and think nothing but resentment for not accepting by Congress, or assigning reasons for not accepting the cession of this State, will operate against it. Our people still retain their opinions of the importance of this State, its superiority in the Union, and the very great exertions and advances it has made in preference to all others. These views are generally local, not seeing the necessity or propriety of general measures now the war is over. These notions are great obstacles to the adoption of the 5 per cent duty as a general revenue.

It is impossible to estimate the individual debt of the State with any precision. By some computations we shall have to provide for raising £300,000 annually, to discharge the interest of our Continental quota and State debt. The Commissioners appointed have settled as far as they were able the expence of the Illinois country. They have discovered great frauds and impositions, and reduced the debt very considerably, but it is still enormous. The accounts are not yet returned, so that I cannot give you the balance. Nathan's demand is referred to the committee of the whole. Strong suspicions prevail against Pollock's integrity, and it is said proofs can be adduced to show the injustice of his

claim

claim upon the State. In short the prejudices here are so great against those who have demands for money or necessaries furnished on the public account to the westward, that it is to be feared injury may result to individuals. At the same time it must be confessed many circumstances authorize a suspicion of the fairness of their claims. A Mr. Pollard formerly of N. York, is just arrived from Bristol. He brings papers so late as the 8th April. An administration appears to have been then formed as was stated in the packet of the last week. North and Fox by the coalition had lost their influence and were generally reprobated. It was doubted whether the last would be re-elected in Westminster. Caermathen was to go to France to put the finishing hand to the treaty, but had not departed, and it was uncertain when he would. The nation exceedingly divided by the Whig and Tory parties about the place. The bill for opening the commerce with America had gone through three different modifications and not likely to pass.*

———

The bill declaring who shall be citizens has not yet been considered in a Committee of the Whole. P. H—y, R. H. L. against any discrimination. I cannot concur, and must, when the matter comes on take part with those who are for some discrimination so as not to trench upon the treaty. A long petition from Essex drawn by M. J. has been presented questioning the right of Congress to make the peace as it stands, asserting the 4th article interferes with

* The text of these bills is printed in the appendix to " Report of a Committee of the Lords of the Privy Council on the trade of Great Britain with the United States, January, 1791."

the

the legislation of the States. Yesterday a petition from Hanover with near 300 subscribers was presented, praying the refugees may not be allowed the right of citizenship. I am pretty confident there is a majority of the House in favor of the sentiments of the last petition.*

JONES TO MADISON.

RICHMOND, 14th June, 1783.

DEAR SIR,

I have your favour of the 3d and 6th with the papers inclosed. Since my last the plan of revenue recommended by Congress has been considered in a Committee of the Whole, and the result contained in the inclosed resolutions, which were agreed to without a division, the number appearing in support of the plan of Congress being so few as not to require it. Mr. B—xt—n and young Mr. Nelson only supported it. In the course of the debate Mr. R. H. L. and Mr. C. M. T. spoke of Congress, having a right to borrow and make requisitions that were binding upon the States, ought also to concert the means for accomplishing the end was reprobated in general as alarming and of dangerous tendency. In short some of the sentiments in the letter to Rhode Island, through argumentative only, operated so powerfully on peoples' mind here, that nothing could induce them to adopt the manner recommended by Congress for obtaining revenue.† If the 5 per cent. is granted to be credited to the State's quota, which is the

---

* An undated half leaf laid with the preceding letter.

† Prepared by Hamilton, and printed in his works (Lodge's edition), vol. II, p. 3, and also in the Journals of Congress, April 24, 1783.

prevailing

prevailing opinion, it will defeat that revenue, unless all the States consent, and N. H., Connecticut, Jersey and N. Carolina never will I expect agree to it. Our people have great jealousy of Congress and the other States; think they have done more than they ought, and that the U. S. owe them at least one million pounds. These notions they will not relinquish though they acknowledge they are not ready to settle the account. After the two first resolutions had passed, P. H. separated from R. H. L. and his party, and warmly supported the granting the duties to Congress and the other revenue to make up this State's quota. I will make an attempt to obtain the 5 per cent. as a general revenue, and to authorize the payment of the other revenue by the collectors to the Continental receiver, instead of the State treasurer. If these can be effected the funds will be on a tolerable footing but for the delay which a departure from the plan of Congress must occasion.

The disposition to oblige the officers of our lines with land beyond the Ohio in the room of those on Cumberland, which are said to be insufficient and very generally barren, has occasioned several leading members to press for withdrawing our cession to Congress, that no obstacle might remain to gratifying the officers. Hitherto we have been lucky enough to delay a determination, which however cannot be many more days postponed. A. L.* proposed a resolution two days ago to withdraw it; an amendment was proposed to fix a time (the 1st September next), when it should stand revoked if not accepted by Congress. The committee rose without coming to a resolution. Something of this sort will I think ultimately take place. If a secret

---

* Arthur Lee.

instruction

instruction to our delegates was practicable to relax, if necessary, any of the conditions, I should like it, as I wish heartily to relinquish that country to the United States. The expence attending that country I shall soon know, as the Commissioners who have been sent to settle the accounts are just returned.

The proposed alteration for ascertaining the proportions of the States, from the conversations I have had with gentlemen on the subject, will be approved. I entertain, however, no sanguine expectation of anything I hear in conversation since the great majority against the plan of revenue, which, from conversation when I first arrived, I was led to believe would be adopted. Many now say the reading the pamphlet of Congress determined them against the measure, disapproving the sentiments conveyed in the letter to Rhode Island.

You cannot well conceive the deranged state of affairs in this Country. There is nothing like system; confusion and embarrassment ever attend such a state of things. The two great commanders make excellent harangues, handsome speeches to their men, but they want executive officers, or should be more so themselves, to be useful. Indeed, so far as I am able to judge from the short time I have been here, we are much in want of useful men, who do business as well as speak to it. A Pendleton and Jefferson would be valuable acquisitions to this Assembly. We want too a Fitzsimons,* or some men of his mercantile knowledge and experience.

The citizen bill remains in the situation as when I last wrote. Before we rise, it is probable something may be

---

*Of Pennsylvania.

done

done in it, especially if the definitive treaty arrives, which it is probable, as a ministry has been formed will soon take place. To divest those who appeared to oppose the payment of the British debts from any attempt of that sort so repugnant to the article of the treaty, and as an alternative less offensive, I have intimated that it would be better to give an instruction to our commissioners for settling the treaty of commerce to propose a suspension of payment for some years, to make it more convenient to the debtors, and it is probable something may be done in that way as an instruction to our delegates in Congress. In Committee on the State of the Commonwealth yesterday, nothing in consequence of the arbitration was taken up, but Mr. N—l—s insisting there was a Committee in town employed in settling the accounts against the public of the Illinois country who could give information about that claim and show there had been fraud in the transaction, the Committee rose without coming to a conclusion. It is to be brought on again to day, when the commissioner (Col. Fleming) is to be examined. It is expected great impositions have taken place in Pollock's affair, which is also before the House and to come up next Tuesday.

I have sold my chariot, and I think shall my phaeton; in which case, and if I get the money for them, I may spend two or three months this fall in Philadelphia, as I must get a carriage made there. Of this you shall be informed. Compliments to Bland and Mercer; hope they will be content to receive from you an account of what we are doing, if not otherwise informed.

JONES TO MADISON.

RICHMOND, 21st June, 1783.

DEAR SIR,

Yours of the 10th I have duly received by the post this week.   We are now as usual putting to sleep many of the bills that have employed our time and attention for great part of this session.   Among them two, one for the benefit of debtors, the other for regulating the proceedings in the County Courts.   These were thought to have some connection and ought to rest together.   Mr. Mason introduced and patronized the debtors bill.   I was not in the House when it was read, but understand it allowed all creditors to obtain judgment, but suspended execution, [or] rather permitted it for a fifth of the debt annually, for five years, comprehending as well foreign as domestic credits.   I came into the House during the debate and from the observations of R. H. L. and those who opposed the bill, its principle was severely reprobated.   Mr. Mason and C. M. T. warmly supported it and pronounced it indispensably necessary to preserve the people from ruin and the country independent. The disposition of the members however was so prevalent for lopping off all business not really necessary that the latter gentlemen were obliged to submit to its being referred to the next session.   This bill, at least so far as respected British creditors, would have had more advocates but for the late period at which it was introduced, and because there already existed and will continue in force until the 1st of December a law that prohibits suits for or on account of British subjects.

The bill granting revenue to Congress to discharge this State's quota of the common debt was taken into consideration

ation yesterday, but being very imperfect was postponed until Monday next. My endeavors to get the impost granted as a general revenue will be fruitless, so universal is the opposition to giving it otherwise than to be credited to the State. The collection too must be by the naval officer, and by him paid to the Continental receiver quarterly. The land tax is to be collected by the sheriffs and paid into the treasury, and by him to the Continental receiver — the deficiency, if any, to be made up out of the poll tax. If the impost was general, these funds would be adequate. Our people will not submit the collectors to be amenable to Congress. If both collections were to be paid to the Continental receiver, the bond given payable to Congress, and judgments to be moved for by the Continental receiver, the revenue could not be well diverted to any other purposes, and would answer the object, and nearly come up to the plan of Congress. Duplicate receipts or settlements might be lodged with the treasurer of the amount of the revenues by the respective collectors, and the State thereby informed of the proceeds annually, independent of the general communication from Congress.

The letter of the delegates and the report of the committee respecting the cession have been read and referred to a Committee of the Whole. This not being the act of Congress a disposition prevails not to take it up. If we have time and the members patience to do it, I shall press its being taken up and the delegates fully instructed to close the matter with Congress, if to be effected, or the cession [to] be void by a certain day; and this I would have fixed to some day after the meeting of the next session. The accounts from the Illinois are before the executive and a committee

mittee of the House appointed to inspect them. They are at present incomplete and any formation of the balance must be altogether conjecture or I should mention it.

A bill has passed the Delegates establishing funds for paying the interest and sinking the principal of the debt due to our line of the army for pay and depreciation, including the State troops. Eight years are allowed for extinguishing the debt. 9d on salt, 4d on wine, 4d on spirits, with some imposts on malt liquor and a duty of 10s per hogshead on tobacco exported, are the funds which are thought adequate to pay the interest and extinguish the principal in that time. The deficiency, if any, is to come out of the poll tax. We have an empty treasury or so nearly so as not to have sufficient to pay the delegates their wages; and the collection of the taxes being postponed, I think the civil list and delegates to Congress will be reduced to difficulties. I forgot to mention above, that the report of the committee on the cession has not fully removed the fears of our people respecting Indian purchases and grants to companies. Their jealousy of Congress on that head is very strong.

Mr Lee tells me he sets out to day for Philadelphia. I expect he will be a fortnight at least before he reaches the city. I may spend two or three months there this fall. The new arrangement of the British ministry, one would think, cannot last long. Like oil and water jumbled together they will soon separate. Their existence will I hope be extended to the accomplishment of the definitive treaty. Hartley appears to have been a friend to its conclusion. Several of the banished Scotsmen and some refugees have returned to this State; three or four to Petersburg of the former, whose presence has so provoked the
people

people of that neighborhood that they were to meet yesterday to order them away. The citizen bill stands the order of the day for Monday. The opponents of this bill think it premature, as the definitive treaty has not appeared. They also assert it to be unwise and impolitic to refuse the admission of these or any others disposed to settle in the country. A discrimination will, however, if the business is brought on, take place, with respect to refugees whatever may be the fate of the banished merchants. The settlement of this business is the more necessary as there is a very severe law in force against British subjects and those who have left the country and joined them, which will not I think be repealed, unless the citizen bill be taken up. This with the revenue bill for the Continental debt, the cession, the alteration proposed in ascertaining the quota of each State, and Nathan's demand, which is to come on next Monday, are the principal matters remaining to be considered, and will be finished in the course of the next week. I shall leave Richmond this day week. Your letters after the receipt of this please to direct to Fredericksburg. Monroe will send Mr. Jefferson his letter.

JONES TO MADISON.

RICHMOND, 28th June, 1783

DEAR SIR,

I have your favours by the post and by the Secretary of War. The day before yesterday the bill for granting a revenue to Congress upon the 3d reading was ordered to lay upon the table. Taz—ll then moved for leave to bring in another under a different title, which was agreed to, and

yesterday

yesterday it was presented and on the first reading postponed to the next session of Assembly. The first bill was imperfectly drawn and had undergone such alterations as to be thought unfit to be enacted into a law. It granted the 5 per cent impost and the duty on enumerated articles, not as a general fund but to be carried to the credit of the state and to be in force if Maryland, Pennsylvania and North Carolina adopted the impost. It granted the land tax, and if any deficiency, the poll tax, to furnish the quota of this state of the 1,500,000 dollars; the first to be collected by the naval officers, the latter by the sheriffs; the whole appropriated to Congress on account of this State's quota of the common debt. The latter bill was drawn to grant the impost duty as a general fund, the collection under the controul of the Executive, but to be paid to the Continental receiver for the use of Congress. The reason of this bill being brought before the House in that form was the apparent change in many members after discussing the first bill to fall in with the proposition of Congress except as to the mode [of] collecting. This conciliatory disposition was much improved by the arrival of a letter from Genl. Washington on the subject, which the Speaker received just before the question was about to be taken on the first bill, and being read in consequence of the consent of the House to hear the letter before the question was taken, had a good effect. But two days alone remaining of the time allotted by the members for finishing the business, and the fixed determination to break up at that day (Saturday) suspended all hope of accomplishing any thing effectual this season. I think if the members could have been prevailed on to continue a week longer the business would have been finished nearly to the wish of Congress.

This

This session has passed over without doing anything of consequence. Yesterday I suggested to the House an idea with respect to the cession; to instruct the delegates to recede from the guarantee provided Congress would agree to the other conditions and limit the time (some time in November next) when they should accept, or the cession stand revoked. It will be vain to attempt relaxing the clause respecting the companies. The other parts of the report of the last committee appear to be agreeable here. The Secretary of War yesterday through the Executive laid before the House a request to be empowered to procure for the United States about ten acres of land for the purpose of establishing a magazine. A bill is ordered for the purpose. Resolutions are to be presented to-day for furnishing Congress a place of residence. Williamsburg, the public buildings and lands, or a tract of territory opposite George Town, as may be most agreeable, with a large sum to erect hotels for the delegates, and other necessary buildings, will be offered in full sovereignty. Liberal as the offer of Maryland has been our people seem disposed not to be backward in surpassing that liberality where they think a lasting benefit may result to the community. I wish they could have seen the place of Congress in the same light and have acted with equal policy and liberality of sentiment.

This day closes the session. I intend [to go] to Mr. Randolph's this evening on my way home, where I have not yet been. The heat of the weather and this infernal hole at this season of the year have almost laid me up. Although Virginia may not grant the funds for discharging their quota of the common debt in the manner desired by Congress, they are I think determined to furnish ample

revenues

revenues for the purpose. Mr Laurens gives us no hope of speedily obtaining the definitive treaty. Nothing has been done in the citizen bill; it lies over, and a severe law against British subjects coming into this country remains in force. The executive may by a proper use of this law until the next session keep out such as ought not to come among us. After getting home you shall be informed when I shall see you in Philadelphia. Joe is yet afflicted with the spleen and ought to go to the Springs or up the country. If John Dawson will accompany Mrs. Jones and Joe up the country, I do not know but I may visit for two or three months the city of Philadelphia during the sickly season.

JONES TO MADISON.

FREDERICKSBURG, 14th July, 1783.

DEAR SIR,

Your favour of the 30th ult. I have duly received, giving the history of the proceedings that brought about the removal of Congress to Princeton. That two of the members of the committee were disposed to advise the President to the measure which his inclination encouraged them to adopt, I have no doubt; but why so important a step should rest with the committee and the president, I am at a loss to comprehend, unless Congress were so intimidated by the conduct of the soldiery as to fear mischievous consequences from their coming together, and so left the business to the committee and the president. Mr. H.'s excuse for concurring in the measure is by no means satisfactory. To be indifferent in a matter of such consequence, or to yield
oneself

oneself up to the guidance of others is a conduct in my judgment reprehensible and has precipitated that body into a situation I apprehend not very agreeable, as well as exposed them to censure and ridicule. Although judging by the event is not a fair conclusion, it is but too commonly the case, and on the present occasion will give force to the censures of those who wish to divert them from the Executive of the State, who from the report of the committee were jointly blameable for declining to give those assurances of support which the circumstances of the case and the dignity of government required. I wish Congress had shown more firmness in their conduct with respect to the soldiery; especially as no just cause of personal danger presented itself, and had remained in Philadelphia, notwithstanding the refusal of support by the Executive, and have afterwards taken up the matter of indignity and disrespect on the part of the State with temper and coolness, and have made that the ground of   removal to one of the places tendered them by the other States. The public opinion would have gone with them more generally than as the affair has been conducted. They are now thought to have been too timid, at the same time that the Executive are blamed for their remissness. To return to Philadelphia is I suppose now out of the question. Princeton, I presume, cannot long serve the purpose. Where then will you fix? Pray inform me what is likely to be done in the matter, and how you are accommodated in Princeton. If I visit you, can a tolerable berth be procured? The sickly season is approaching and if I move at all it will be in about a fortnight or three weeks, especially if the treasurer could furnish the needful. Mr. L. we hear

is

is to be minister for foreign affairs. Heaven smiles upon us this year as the crops are in general very promising.

JONES TO MADISON.

SPRING HILL, 21ˢᵗ July, 1783

DEAR SIR,

I find mine to you of the last week was not in town in time for the mail, which it seems is now made up at ten in the forenoon, and is rather inconvenient for those of the country near the town, as they cannot receive and answer letters the same week unless in town. My letter will I presume go forward this week. I did suppose Congress would not again return to the city, and should be sorry to hear they had done so unless invited, or some step taken by the Executive to atone for the slight put on that body. Had I been present, I should have opposed the removal at the time; but having done so and [for] the cause assigned, I should not consent to return until some concession or act of contrition on the part of the offenders authorized the measure. The act of the Executive must be deemed the act of the State until disclaimed or censured by the supreme authority, and it is not probable this will be the consequence considering the composition of the present Assembly, unless this conduct of Mr. D. should lessen the attachment of some of his adherents.

I know not yet whether I shall visit Congress. If I do I shall depart hence the beginning of next month. I shall feel the inconvenience of the removal in the want of some good accommodations, as I hoped and expected to get at my friend Mrs. House's, where if Congress have returned

or

or shall return I depend upon quarters, of which the next post shall convey notice. The proclamation of the Executive has, I am told, given offence to the B. party, and threats have been thrown out of calling for the Council Book next session with a view to censure the advisers of the measure. I am no prophet but will venture to foretell that the person who attempts it will fail in his project and meet rather the censure than applause of the people. If the definitive treaty arrives before the meeting in the fall, I expect we shall have a long and warm session.

JONES TO MADISON.

SPRING HILL, 28th July, 1783.

DEAR SIR,

Yours of the 7th inst. came duly to hand. It is strange we have yet no satisfactory accounts of the definitive treaty. The settlement of a British ministry, I hoped, would have speedily brought that important matter to a close; but for anything we are at present informed, the time of its completion is very uncertain. Has any step been taken on our part towards a treaty of commerce? They seem to have moved cautiously in that business. Surely we shall not be precipitate who are, compared to Britain, but novices, very young actors on the theater of commerce.

I recollect not giving any intimations to your friends that it would be inconvenient for you to take part in the legislative concerns next fall. On the contrary, I think I rather encouraged the notion, or at least left it quite free for your choice, as I hoped and still wish it may suit you to give us your assistance at that time.

I hope

9 *

I hope such of the leaders of the late mutiny as shall appear to be guilty, will meet the punishment due to their crimes. Some of the officers of that line (I mean, P^a.) are, if we are to judge from former transactions, old offenders, and having before been pardoned for similar misconduct, are the less entitled to favor now. It is to be regretted those principally concerned have escaped. I doubt whether it would be proper for Congress to return to Philadelphia even upon an address to the citizens, unless couched in terms expressive of the disapprobation of the conduct of the executive and willingness then as well as at all future times when properly required to turn out in support of the dignity of the federal government [which has] (if the report of the committee deserves credit, and we have no reason to doubt any part of it) been grossly disregarded by the executive authority of the State. I think at present I should reluctantly return upon the proposed address and not willingly until the Legislature by some proper resolution paved the way. The treasurer still leaves me in suspense. Whether to morrow's post will produce anything that will prepare the way to my return I cannot now inform you. If I should revisit the city my hopes still are I shall see you before your departure.

JONES TO MADISON.

SPRING HILL, 4th August 1783.

DEAR SIR,

The last post brought me a letter from the treasurer which determines my visit to Congress. He informs me he has bills to the amount of upwards of twelve hundred pounds

pounds on Philadelphia which he wishes to apply to the use of the delegation and had written to you and also to me informing us of it, that our correspondents, and those of the other gentlemen, might obtain warrants for our respective proportions of them. He says he requested your answer by the last or this post. I have desired Col. Monroe to obtain a warrant on my account. If not done, the other gentlemen will direct their correspondents to do the same that the bills may be forwarded without delay. Should they arrive before I get up, you will be pleased to receive my proportion. I am not certain of the day, but within a week or ten days at farthest I shall, health permitting, set out. If Congress should be returned to Philadelphia, I require a room at Mrs. House's; if at Princeton they still remain, your assistance to procure me one shall be thankfully acknowledged. Although I think were I present my voice would be opposed to returning to the city for reasons formerly assigned, yet I must confess being in Philadelphia will best suit me on account of some private matters I have to attend to, as well as on account of more convenient accommodation—an object of some consideration to me in my uncertain health and advanced years. I shall return my carriage from Baltimore, that Mrs. Jones and Joe may visit the upper country if she chooses to do so, rather than hazard continuing during the sickly season on Rappahannock. From Baltimore, I shall ride, or take the stage, as upon inquiry I shall think most agreeable. This quarter affords no news for your entertainment.

JONES TO MADISON.

SPRING HILL, 30th October, 1783.

DEAR SIR,

After two or three interruptions on the road by rainy weather, I arrived here the 23^d tolerably well. Two days after Mr. Hardy and Monroe called on me on their way to Philadelphia, by whom you will receive this. They hope to find Congress in the city by the time they get up, but by your communication received by the post this week I gave them little encouragement to be so happily situated. It gives me concern to find such indirect methods practiced to carry points, and though in the end George Town should be solely established the seat of Congress, instead of their alternate residence, much as I prefer that place, I should not be very well pleased with the manner of its being accomplished.

Although the conduct of Congress with respect to the western country may call forth the resentment of some of the Legislature of Virginia, yet I trust there will be a sufficient number to close with the terms transmitted by Congress, and thereby terminate the disagreeable and dangerous controversy so warmly supported by some of the States against ours on the right to that country. My endeavors to procure its passage shall not be wanting as I consider the ground on which the cession is now placed beneficial to the State, and by proper management may prove very much so to the United States.

From the temper of the Eastern States with respect to the commutation, if nothing else operated with them, I entertained very slender hopes of their adopting the plan of Congress. The rejection of it by Massachusetts was no

more

more than I expected as well on that account, as from some
other motives that are sufficiently known to you. Have
they laid taxes to pay their quota of the national debt by
any other mode than the one recommended? or have they
in fact refused the Commissioner appointed to settle the
public accounts permission to proceed upon that business?
Notwithstanding these obstacles I still wish Virginia to
agree to the proposition and hope to find the Legislature
disposed to do so. I set off in a few days for Richmond.
Company has hitherto prevented me since my arrival from
putting up the things you desired and sending them to Mr.
Maury. It shall be done before I leave home. Mr. Jefferson must be with you as the gentlemen here inform me he
had gone on the upper road. Remember me respectfully
to him and all inquiring friends, particularly to the good
lady of the house, and Mrs. Trist, if she is still with you.
Tell her Joe says he remembers and thanks her for the
sword she was so kind as to send him. The vessel on board
which I put my things is not yet arrived. I fear she was
out in the storm that happened the Saturday night and
Sunday morning I left you.

JONES TO JEFFERSON.

RICHMOND, 21 December, 1783

DEAR SIR,

I have your favor by the post this week and have the
satisfaction to inform you the Assembly have passed a law
granting the impost to Congress. Also that a bill has
passed the delegates, and is now before the Senate, accepting the terms stipulated by Congress respecting the western
lands,

lands, and authorizing the delegates to convey the claim of this State to the United States. I have no doubt of its passing the Senate, though I fear they will attempt to restore a clause which on the third reading was struck out by the delegates, whereby a further condition was annexed, that a quantity of land sufficient to comply with the resolves of the two Houses granting lands to certain persons, should be reserved. The delegates upon reflection thought it better to put a finishing hand to this business than hazard further altercation and perhaps the final settlement of so important an object and therefore parted (?) from the clause. That the Senate, some of whom are much attracted to those for whom the clause provided, might not restore it by amendment, I have mentioned to a few of them as a better and less exceptionable mode, the instructing our delegates to move in Congress for such an allowance of land out of that ceded as may enable the State to fulfill their engagements. This course will probably be taken. We had passed a law empowering the Congress to prohibit if they thought fit, the entry of British vessels into our ports, or to adopt any other mode they preferred to counteract the designs of Great Britain on our commerce, so long as they should adhere to their present system. Your letter to the Governor intimating your apprehensions the business will not be speedily done by Congress, as they can only recommend. We meant by publishing our resolves on the subject to call the immediate attention of the States to it, that similar measures might be taken by them. The plan of counteracting the British policy I could wish should proceed from Congress in consequence of powers to be communicated for that purpose, to exhibit to that nation an instance that

the

the States are not so jealous of that body as to withhold powers that are necessary whenever the general welfare presents the occasion, and to convince them of their error that we cannot in this business act in concert. The transmission of our act to the Executives of the several States with request that their attention may be immediately called to this great object, may produce similar acts on their part and expedite the plan of opposition. We expected to rise to day, but think at present we shall not accomplish it.

N. B. Mr H—y, who at first proposed to instruct the delegates to press for sessions from the other States, at length relinquished the design for the reason you mention — the disagreeable predicament in which we would place our delegates.

JONES TO JEFFERSON.

FREDERICKSBURG, 29ᵗʰ December, 1783

DEAR SIR,

I have the satisfaction to inform you the Senate contrary to my expectation passed the act authorizing the Delegates in Congress to convey the claim of Virginia to the territory northwestward of the Ohio to the United States, without amendment, and it will be transmitted you without the instruction heretofore intimated. The mode adopted for transferring our right was in pursuance and in conformity to the precedent established by New York in her cession. Perhaps an act vesting the claim of this State in the United States might have been more proper and less troublesome; but as there was a precedent, it was thought better to pursue *that*, than adopt a contrary method. Some of the
learned

learned judges (but not of the Chancery) doubted the efficacy of such deed of conveyance, as the Congress, not being a corporate body, could not take a title by conveyance. I am so little used to law proceedings of late, and so incompetent a judge of difficult cases without recurring to books, that the objection had not struck me, and I do not now feel so strongly as they appeared to do, the force of the objection — conceiving, as I do, the cession to be a conventional act between sovereign and independent States, and not to be scanned by the rules of municipal law. I mention this circumstance that if you think there is weight in it the necessary precaution may be observed.

I think I before informed you we had granted the impost duties with some conditions similar to those of Massachusetts. Another perhaps would have been proper, and had it occurred in time would probably have been inserted in the act for determining questions of seizures for small value in the County Courts, rather than compelling persons in all cases to defend themselves in the Court of Admiralty in Williamsburg. Should this in practice be found oppressive, as it reaches not the substance, I presume it may be redressed. The completing the cession and granting the impost may not improperly be called sacrifices by this State to the common good of the Union, and will, it is to be hoped, lessen, if not wholly suspend the illiberal censures heretofore cast upon us. Add to these the unanimity and spirit with which the legislature passed an act to empower Congress to concert measures to counteract the designs of Great Britain on our commerce — all of them calculated to produce harmony, and strengthen the hands of the Federal government. The impost I assure you was

with

with some a bitter pill, but finding it must be swallowed, they ceased at length to make opposition.

Although we could not doubt the signing of the definitive treaty in terms almost the same as the provisional articles, yet as the same was not ratified and regularly communicated, it was thought proper to continue the   law as it is called for four months, and from thence to the end of the next session of Assembly.   It was strongly contended this would be deemed an infraction of the treaty, but a great majority appeared in favor of continuing the law. From an opinion we were under no obligation to put into a train of execution what was not properly before us.   Pray inform us at your leisure whether any thing and what has been done respecting the negros carried away from New York by the British.   What about the British debts or the interest of them, as I think some instructions were given our Commissioners on the subject, particularly the interest. Have any steps been taken, or proposed to be taken, to obtain information of the amount of the claim of the British creditors on these States, or will it be left to the respective States to pursue their own measures.   If it be true that three millions of pounds sterling, the lowest calculation I have heard of, be due from the citizens of America to the subjects of Great Britain, and probably a much larger sum ; is it within their ability, encumbered as they are with other demands, equally just and pressing, to make prompt payment? If not, should not some negotiation be opened under the authority of Congress, or the respective States to gain knowledge of the amount of the debt, and at what periods by installment the creditors are content to receive payment.   This will be an embarrassing business the next
session

session of Assembly, and is rendered the more so as it involves the payments under the law made into the Treasury during the continuance of the act and draws into consequence all transactions under the tender laws. Were you in the Assembly when the confiscation law passed (I am told you were the draftsman), by which it appears to me the property meant to be confiscated was by the law vested in the Commonwealth, and although not yet sold, may still be so without infringing the treaty, as I conceive the proceeding to complete or take inquisitions for the purpose of designating the property cannot be deemed future confiscations, and I learn there is much property at this time in the predicament I mention. In short, I foresee we shall have great and perplexing questions agitated the next session of Assembly such as call for moderation and wisdom to discuss and settle, and the prospect of the body's possessing abilities equal to the trust, not so promising as I could wish. Madison's aid I think we may depend on; perhaps old Mr. G. Mason's, as the business of the land offices require revision, and his apprehensions on that subject, if nothing else, may draw him from his retirement. Upon these or many other subjects that may fall under our consideration, I shall thank you for your sentiments so far as you think it either proper or prudent to convey them.

JONES TO JEFFERSON.

SPRING HILL, 28th February, 1784.

DEAR SIR,

I have yours of the 2d inst. by Col. Monroe's Adam. I lament his not returning accompanied with the means of relief,

relief, having heretofore experienced the disagreeable as well as disgraceful predicament in which the gentlemen of the delegation are placed for want of remittances from the State. It is to be hoped you have received the small supply the Treasurer mentioned to me he had lately forwarded, and that he will very soon be able to furnish a more ample succour. He has sent me an order for what cash may have been collected by the sheriffs of Spotsylvania and King George of the current taxes. I will obtain what I can under this order and forward it for your relief. As yet the sheriffs have done little owing to the severity of the season, which, instead of abating, is to-day and was yesterday, as cold as almost any time of the winter; and the river, which had opened a little in particular places, again blocked up.

Knowing that instructions had been given our Commissioners on the subject of British debts, and uninformed what had been the issue of the propositions, I supposed Congress might still have it in contemplation to move in that matter. I apprehended the British claim upon America was more than could be discharged by prompt payment, and concluded time for payment indispensably necessary. To judge what time was necessary a knowledge of the amount of the demand appeared to me a pre-requisite; besides it seemed to me to be the most proper course to conduct this business by negotiation between the creditors and debtors or the State in behalf of the debtors, and that the sooner some steps for this purpose were adopted the better. In consequence of these reflections I had prepared a motion the last session of Assembly to be offered the House calculated to obtain information as to the debt, as well as to feel the pulse of the British creditors as to peri-
odical

odical payments. The departure of some of the principal
members and the thinness of the House at the close of the
session, deterred me from offering as it was a proposition
of such importance. I am well satisfied the magnitude of
the debt and the impracticability of speedy payment will
well authorize *ex parte* measures without subjecting us to
the imputation of violating the treaty; and perhaps themselves of equal measures to all our creditors the most eligible. Yet addition of interest of the debt during the war
is a great increase of it if we are liable to pay it. Would
not the mode of negotiating with the creditors be the best
to get rid of that difficulty for it is very probable from all
I can hear the creditors, at least many of them would
be   to secure the principal due when the separation
took place than claim interest during the war. The debts
contracted within the State have near the whole of them
been settled, and mortgages and bonds taken by the factors
at the commencement of the contest; so that a small part
only rests on simple contract. I thought with you and am
yet inclined to that opinion (though I confess I do not
openly espouse it) that the stipulations of the treaty sub-
jected us to pay the interest. Inclining as I do to that
opinion I yet have my doubts. Could British subjects after
the war claim and recover their debts of our citizens? If
they could not, how comes it that a dead debt revived by
the treaty should gather interest during its death or suspension. I speak not here of the moral obligation to pay.
Although I applaud your sentiments respecting confiscated
property and when I get sufficient information of facts respecting the state of that business, may be disposed to be
generous, yet at present I own I feel little propensity to
                                                          be

be so. My inquiry respecting the undisposed confiscations had for its object the more effectually bringing about an accommodation of the payment of the British debts, and is not intended by me for any other purpose unless circumstances, as yet unknown to me, shall alter my sentiments. I think the information from our Commissioners of the transactions of the negotiation gave us reason to think the British Commissioners expect no fruits from the recommendation of Congress. Old Franklin overpowered them on the question by a candid offer to go into a fair settlement of the accounts, which was declined. As soon as I receive the treasurers account of the confiscated property I will inform you of it. Your letter to Capt. Hays which went to Buchanan in Richmond is returned by my servant. I have sent it to Maury, to be forwarded to Madison, who will take care of it. I fear you will be puzzled to read my bad writing; it is really so cold I can scarce hold my pen.

JONES TO MADISON.

RICHMOND, 30 March, 1785.

DEAR SIR,

I have your favor by Col. Richᵈ. Taylor. The letter for the Attorney has been delivered and he is informed when Mr. Taylor will leave town. Mr. Maier some time past made application to the Executive, and laid before them a state of his case. Although it was not altogether satisfactory he had a legal demand against the State, yet the circumstances were in general so favorable to his pretensions, he obtained for his present relief £150, and an assurance that

that his case would be laid before the Assembly.* The other matter has not yet come forward. I will enquire into Mr. Maier's situation, and if I shall find your aid necessary will apply it. On my return from King George I found a letter here from Monroe to you, which I forwarded by way of Fredericksburg to the care of Mr. Maury. No other has since appeared. Indeed nothing very important had been decided, though many things of moment were depending. J. Adams is appointed minister to Court of London, outvoting R. R. Livingston and Rutledge: Adams 8, Livingston 3, Rutledge 2; the first vote, Adams 6, Livingston 5, Rutledge 2. Virginia and Maryland at first voted for L. but went over to A. finally. Jefferson it is expected will remain in France. By a letter from Short lately received by W. Nelson, Jefferson was about to visit London. Whether merely a private trip or to meet Adams is not mentioned; but I suppose a private visit as Adam's appointment could not have reached him. Gardoqui is coming to America to adjust matters respecting our boundary with Spain. G. W. is reduced to difficulties respecting his acceptance of the shares in the companies. Inclosed you have a copy of the act. Short writes that Berkeley had postponed executing the order for the bust until the return of the Marquis, that the likeness might be taken more perfectly. We have sent by way of N. York to the care of the delegates the resolution of the last session, and the first vessel from here will carry a duplicate. The president of Congress in his letter of last week says they have reason to think the dispute between the Emperor and the United Provinces will be accommodated. He says there appears a

* See Madison to Jefferson, 27 April, 1785. (Madison's Writings, I., 145.)

disposition

disposition on the part of G. Britain to settle the difficulties between them and the U. States respecting the treaty and other matters, *if by our conduct on this side the water we do not prevent it.* He says also measures are taking and in great forwardness for holding a conference with the S. tribes of Indians for the purpose of accommodating matters with them. I observe by the treaty the Shawanese are not parties; it is said they were prevailed on by British emissaries not to attend.

I have this day removed to the house where Capt. Seabrook's family now live and have the two rooms up stairs, such as they are, and the entertaining room below. He has already, and the rest of the family are by the 1st May, to remove for the summer into the country, so that I am to occupy the house until I leave the town about 1st July, with the furniture in it. If you come to town for the Court, which I think you said you intended, I desire you will come here, as you can have a bed and other accommodations, though not so well as we could wish, yet so as to be tolerably comfortable. Pray do not scruple to give orders on me for the money I owe you, as I can accommodate you.

JONES TO MADISON.

RICHMOND, 12 June, 1785.

DEAR SIR,

Being from town when your order for the trunk arrived was the reason it was not then sent. If an opportunity offers, it shall be forwarded as you desire. In the mean time the precaution of preserving the cloaths from the moth by exposing them to the sun has been attended to

and

and shall be repeated. I know not whether any copy of the resolution you allude to has been officially communicated to Mr. Mason. Such as Beckley copied for the Executive have been, so whether *that* should have been of the number I cannot tell as we are not yet favored with the Journals by the printer, and I cannot inform myself at the clerk's office, Mr. Beckley being out of town. He will, I am told, return to-morrow. If the attorney has not sent I will contrive you the copies you desire. I heard, but have only heard, that Mason and Henderson proceeded to execute the other branch of the business committed to the Commissioners without the attendance or call for attendance of the other Commissioners.* What they have done has not come to my knowledge.

I have determined to leave Richmond the first week of the next month for King George, where I shall stay only a few days, and then proceed towards the Berkeley Springs, to return the beginning of October. At one time I had a notion of going to Rhode Island being much pressed to it by Mrs. Lightfoot near Port Royal, whose husband is in bad health and is advised to make a water trip to that place, and his wife is determined to attend him; but had I gone, we were to have taken our route by land and meet him there. After some reflection I declined the northern for the western trip, whether prudently I cannot tell. But my little boy must accompany me, and I thought the springs on that account most proper. If I pass through Orange and you are in the county, I shall certainly do myself the

---

*Mason and Henderson, on the part of Virginia, and Chase and Jenifer, on the part of Maryland, were commissioners to determine the navigation and jurisdiction of the Potomac River below the falls.

pleasure

pleasure of seeing you. H—r—n succeeded in Surry, where he offered after being disappointed in Charles City.* It is thought there will be a struggle for the chair.

What do you think of an alteration in the Articles or Confederation to vest the Congress with power to regulate trade and collect imposts, to be credited the respective States? The States having staples will not I expect relish it, and yet the necessity of Congress possessing the power is at present apparent. Perhaps a convention of deputies from the several States for the purpose of forming commercial regulations similar to the British navigation act to be carried into execution by Congress, would be the most likely mode to obtain success to the measure, as well as collecting the wisdom of the States on the subject, which is unquestionably of the first importance.†

JONES TO MADISON.

RICHMOND, 23ᵈ June, 1785.

DEAR SIR,

Mr. Beckley has at length furnished me with a copy of the resolution you lately requested might be sent to you. I confide it to the care of Mr. Maury of Fredericksburg,

---

* "The late Govʳ. Harrison, I hear, has been baffled in his own county but meant to be a candidate in Surry, and in case of a rebuff there, to throw another die for the borough of Norfolk. I do not know how he construes the doctrine of residence. It is surmised that the machinations of Tyler, who fears a rivalship for the chair, are at the bottom of his difficulties. (Madison to Jefferson, 27 April, 1785.) Though Harrison removed to Surry with his family, an attempt was made to throw him out, and in the Committee on Privileges an adverse decision was had by the casting vote of the chairman; but on a vote in the House he retained his seat by a very small majority — less than six votes.

† For Madison's views on this subject consult his letter to Monroe of 7th August, 1785.

in

10 *

in hopes it will get safe and soon to your hands. Mr. Blair tells me a copy of this resolution has been transmitted to the State of Maryland, but knows nothing further of the matter. Perhaps the clerk or speaker sent one to Mr. Mason. It would seem necessary something should be done in it previous to the meeting of the Assembly. My determination is to be in King George by the 8th or 10th next month, where I shall stay a few days before I set out on my trip to Berkeley. I should be glad to hear from you and if you mean to leave Orange, which way you bend your course.

JONES TO JEFFERSON.

RICHMOND, 21st February, 1786.

DEAR SIR,

Mr. Madison having given you before he left Richmond a history of the proceedings of the Assembly during their late session, I have only to add to what he has done some particular acts passed by them, a perusal of which may prove more satisfactory than a partial account of them. With these you will receive a small pamphlet entitled "Reflections, &c." ascribed to Mr. St. G. Tucker, together with the proceedings of the Convention of the Protestant Episcopal Church, held lately in Philadelphia, and some newspapers containing a variety of questions respecting our commerce, making in the whole the only report I am at present able to furnish you.

The act for establishing certain ports for foreign vessels passed some time ago, commences its operation the first of June next. It is imperfect, and an attempt was made by a

bill

bill introduced the last session to amend its defects, but was lost in its progress through the Legislature. The operation of this imperfect law it is to be feared will increase the opposition to the measure and work a repeal the next session. I wish a fair experiment could be made to ascertain the advantages or disadvantages of restricting foreign commerce to a few ports. Although its policy is strongly opposed, yet I incline to think upon fair experiment the measure would prove beneficial and establish itself from its fruits. Doubtless it would greatly aid the collection of impost revenue, and suppress these evasions which are now too generally practised by the subtile and interested trader.

A wretched combination of unimformed members, without an individual to utter their objections of the least pretensions to science except M—r—w—r S—th,* proved too powerful for reason and eloquence in favor of the bill for establishing Circuit Courts. Nothing, I think, effectual has been done to counteract the commercial policy of Britain respecting the States. Commissioners to meet commissioners of other States have been appointed. Whether they will ever meet, or when met effect any good purpose is yet in the womb of time. Better far it would have been to confide to Congress such powers as were adequate and necessary to secure and protect our commerce from the attempts of monopoly and the injuries of inequality. If it· is ever to be wrested from the present engrossers of it, the federal power alone can effect [it].

Has anything been done with Britain respecting commerce? Are we to expect a surrender of the posts on the Lakes? The holding of them and declining to account for

---

* Meriwether Smith.

the

the negros carried from New York have served with our people as pretexts for continuing in force the law that prohibits British subjects suing for their debts. Are we to ascribe the reluctance in many instances and the absolute neglect in others, of the Indian tribes, to meet and treat with our Commissioners, to the detention of the posts on the Lakes, or to British and Spanish intrigues with those nations?

Col. le Maire will I expect deliver you this with its inclosures. I wish I could have regaled you with something more entertaining. You must accept the will for the deed. Tobacco is still low; 22s. 6d. last price here. Some think this is owing to a contract made with the Farmers general, the fulfillment of which we are told rests with R. Morris. If Mr. Short is with you, present him my compliments.

Will it be improper to publish in Paris from the Virginia paper, the act concerning G. W.? Le Maire will bear the act of naturalisation to the Marquis.

JONES TO MADISON.

RICHMOND, 30ᵗʰ May, 1786.

DEAR SIR,

Before the receipt of your favour by Maj. Moore I had procured from Mr. Beckley copies of the bill you wanted, and you will receive them enclosed. Something is indispensably necessary to be done respecting the Courts of Justice, or they will soon become grievances instead of giving relief for administering justice. Each of them is already overcharged with business; the general court much behind; the Court of Appeals only trying one cause in a week

week after convening, owing it is said to the lawyers being worn down with laborious attendance on the preceding courts and unable to prosecute the business. The Attorney and Mr. Baker, however, found it convenient to set out the Monday after the Court rose for Williamsburg, to defend some client in the court of admiralty where I suppose the fees were more tempting than in the chancery court. The Attorney was indeed in bad health before the Court broke up, being scarcely able to speak loud enough to be heard, and was compelled for want of voice, which a severe cold deprived him of, to relinquish the business in Williamsburg before it was finished, and since his return has been very ill. He is now better, took the air in his chariot yesterday, but [is] in such a state of health as to require much caution to steer clear of danger. He has had several blisters on him and at this time can speak only in whispers. I think this attack will make him more cautious in future, and not so freely venture health for the sake of money. Mr. Nicholas, I am told, is for district courts on a plan different from any hitherto proposed. I am more and more disposed to concur in the business of districts upon some such plan as White and myself in conversation with you one evening concurred in and for which purpose he was to propose an amendment to the bill before the House. But I never heard further yet.

I sincerely wish you an agreeable journey to the north when you undertake it, and as sincerely wish you success in any speculation you may make on the Mohawk, but confess to you, though I am a stranger to the land and its conveniences, the remoteness from navigation, the long winters and the present uncertain issue of what course the back

commerce

commerce may take leave the advantages of holding lands *there* doubtful to an inhabitant of New York, much more so to a citizen of Virginia. However, nothing can so well clear up these difficulties as a visit to the country and obtaining the best information the present state of things will afford. One caution I will recommend, and that is not to purchase land from any person without first examining it or having it examined by the one you can rely on for true information. I take it for granted those of the country know the value of property there as well perhaps better than others, and generally speaking there are always men to be found ready to obtain what we may call bargains and that N. York have such men in it, able also to buy I must suppose, and should therefore be backward in buying what others seem not much to desire. I offer these hints with freedom, not wishing to .prevent your speculations there, but to interpose necessary caution in whatever you may do.

I shall see King George county next week and perhaps visit Alexandria before my return. We are about to look into the state of the several naval offices and the mode of conducting the business in them, which we think and I hope will have its use.

The British Minister, we hear, has informed Mr. Adams in answer to his demand of the posts, that America must first pay the debts.

JONES TO MADISON.

RICHMOND, 7 June, 1787.

DEAR SIR,

Since my return to Richmond, which place I left soon after the Governor set out, I have yours of the 27th from Philadelphia.

Philadelphia. Mr. Dortman, who has arrived here within a few days past, informed us your information from New York of other delegates coming forward was well founded, as you had ten States represented when he came away. I entertain hopes from the disposition of the members convened, that harmony will prevail and such improvements of the federal system adopted as will afford us a prospect of peace and happiness. I am, however, strongly impressed with fears that your labours in Convention, though wisely conducted and concluded, will in the end be frustrated by some of the States under the influence of interests operating for particular rather than general welfare. Be this as it may, I cannot doubt but the meeting in Philadelphia will (composed as it is of the best and wisest persons in the Union) establish some plan that will be generally approved.

The Lieutenant-Governor tells me he does and shall continue to write to the Governor* once a week at least. I shall do the same to you if I can furnish any sort of materials for a letter worth communicating. At any rate I may support a correspondence by enclosing you by the newspapers; if I can entertain you with nothing more interesting.

A letter from Mr. A. Lee which the Governor has sent us intimates the propriety of proceeding without delay (if the Executive have any money at their command) to purchase up Continental securities, which are now low, but which he seems to think will (if the Convention do anything that will probably meet the approbation of the States, and the sales of the lands by Congress take place) rapidly rise in value. He says also that other States are doing this

* Edmund Randolph.

while

while it is to be effected on easy terms. I wish for information as to the fact, and your sentiments so far as you conjecture respecting the rise of the value of these papers.

We have forbid any further advances of specie to the Commissioner of the U. S. until we can be assured the proportion of indents will be admitted. Those on the requisition of the last year have been withheld, consequently it is too late for the present collection to furnish a proportion of them; and we understand the construction of the Treasury board of the U. S. is that under the requisitions of '84 and '85, the indents issued under each requisition can be received in payment of each, and none of the one be admitted in the other, and so of the last year, had they come forward; and of the year '85 none to be received but such as were in the hands of the State treasurer the 1st January '87, and of '86, none but such as should be in his hands by the 1st July, '87. This was not, I believe, so understood here by the requisitions, and if they were so intended, which may probably have been the case, a point so material for the States to be acquainted with should have been clearly, and not doubtfully expressed.

We have letters from several of the county lieutenants of the Kentucky district of Indian incursions and depredations, many persons killed and horses carried off; of the families many of them in the frontier coming in, particularly in Jefferson. These letters are sent to the delegates in Congress. We have authorized measures of defense only, well knowing an adherence to the militia law our best policy as a State. But the measures of the United States should go further, whenever there is reason for it. Our informations seem to call for such measures, or I am persuaded

suaded very great distress will attend the Kentucky district.
We hear nothing of or from Mr. Butler, or the commander
of the troops of the U. St: My compliments to the Governor. I beg your excuse as I really had forgot your former request about the 2 books. It shall be attended to
now, but you will inform me where they are to be sent.

JONES TO MADISON.

RICHMOND, 29 June, 1787.

DEAR SIR,

We are not to know the result of your deliberations for
five or six weeks to come, as from accounts your session
will continue until some time in August. Some of your
uxorious members will become impatient from so long ab-
sence from home. How does the Dr. stand it? enjoy himself as usual or cast longing looks towards Richmond.
Mrs. McClurg is and looks well, and will I dare say on his
return prove at least a full match for him. Mrs. Randolph
and the children have, I hope, got up safe. Present her if
you please my compliments. Tell the governor we shall
not venture to speculate in indents or any other Continental
securities. Had we the power and the means to follow a
certain gentleman's advise the adoption of his plan would,
with me at least, required other authority to support it.
We have directed the sale of the tobacco on hand in the
manner as you will see by the enclosed paper, and have
some hopes the price will be advanced nearly to the State
price by the receipt of the interest warrants. *These will
soon answer the purposes of specie.* I am told it has had
the effect to appreciate the warrants 2½ per cent. The
sudden

sudden demand at Petersburg the last week for tobacco in consequence of many arrivals started the price there to 24*s*. 6*d*. which had for some time stood at 22*s*. 6*d*.; here it rose from 23*s*. to 24*s*. I am told at Fredericksburg the price has got to 22*s*. 6*d*.; it has been 20*s*. only. Some how it is kept down here, and will I fear be checked in Petersburg.

We last evening had a letter from the searcher at Alexandria complaining of a rescue from his possession of a schooner he had seized. She is from St Kitts, had entered in Maryland, but was detected in landing at Alexandria some rum (the number of hhd. not mentioned) which occasioned her seizure by the searcher. The communication we have received shews that the people of the town were more disposed to act in opposition to law than support the officer in the execution of his duty. We have directed one of the armed boats to endeavour to recover the vessel which we hear moved towards George Town. We have also called for the names of those who assisted the captain and vessel to escape, and directed the searcher to move for the penalty against those who refused to assist him, when summoned by him to offer their aid. The last post I heard late in the evening, that Mr. Harrison was to set out in the stage in the morning. I sent accounts to him with the two books, requesting he would convey them to you.

Will you send me the 7th Essay on Finance.* Adams book is here, and I can get the reading of it.†

---

*By Pelatiah Webster, a merchant of Philadelphia.
† Defence of the Constitution.

JONES TO MADISON.

RICHMOND, 6th July, 1787.

DEAR SIR,

I have your letter of the 26th ult. The post preceding the arrival of yours brought me a letter from the Governor, inclosing Mr. Wythe's resignation,* when the filling the vacancy made by that Gentleman's departure from Convention was considered, and determined by the executive to be unnecessary. The length of time the Convention had been sitting, and the representation of the State then attending, being within one of the number first appointed, and these gentlemen of established character and approved abilities, were considerations that I believe had weight and governed the determination. Had the supplying Mr. Wythe's place been thought necessary, I have no doubt Mr. Corbin's well-known abilities, and his being on the spot, would have pointed him out to the executive as a proper person. It is supposed by some Dr. McClurg will soon retire. Should that be the case, and the other gentlemen remain I am inclined to think from what formerly passed at the board, they will be deemed a representation competent to the great objects for which they were appointed.

If the Massachusetts Assembly should pursue such measures as from the specimens you mention there is reason to fear they will, the example may probably prove contagious and spread into New Hampshire, whereby the Eastern politics will become formidable, and from the principles which

---

* " Mr. Wythe left us yesterday, being called home by the serious declension of his lady's health."— *Madison to Jefferson,* 6 June 1787.

appear

appear to govern them and the number of adherents, per-nicious consequences are to be apprehended.

Tobacco still rises; the price now current will nearly bring us what the State allowed, and it is probable by next Thursday, the day we have fixed for the sale, we shall find purchasers giving a price for all the upland tobacco at least equal if not higher than the State price. Although the Treasury board refused to take tobacco at the State price, we have been applied to this day by Hopkins to postpone the sale until he can apply to and be directed by them what to do, or allow him to bid for tobacco to the amount of the bills on him, which he says is about 25,000 dollars. All circumstances considered, we agreed he may purchase to the amount of 4,000*l*, to be considered as specie, and to be accompanied with the proper proportion of indents under the requisition of '85.

JONES TO MADISON.

RICHMOND, 23ᵈ July, 1787.

DEAR SIR,

Since my last to you I have been very much indisposed, and until a few days past unable to write or attend to any business. At this time I am barely strong enough to take exercise. Are we likely to have a happy issue of your meeting, or will it pass over without effect? Finding you still continue together our hopes are not lost; my fears, how-ever, I must confess, are rather increased than diminished by the protraction of your session, taking it for granted many and great difficulties have been encountered, as there were many and great to remove before a good system could be be established. We have been amused with your either soon separating or continuing to sit until September. I have nothing to tell you of but that I have been disappointed in my expectation we should get for our tobacco the State price. The James, Appomattox and York have been sold here; the two former at near the State price, the latter some shillings below it. A few both of Rappahannock and Potomac were offered; they sold at a loss of 5*s* or 6*s* a hundred. Seeing no prospect of a better price here for these tobaccos, the committee of Council, who attended the sale to assist the treasurer with their advice postponed the sale, and the Rap: tobaccos are to be sold at Fredericksburg, the 1st next month and the Potomack, at Alexandria, the 6th, being the Monday after Col. Meriwether is appointed to do the business under the direction of two of the Council, Col. Mathews and Genl. Wood, who are to attend. It is hoped a better price will be obtained by selling in the manner proposed.

I shall leave this place about the 3d of next month and keep on towards the mountains for the sake of health. Your future letters, therefore, please to direct to Fredericksburg.

The Virginia Legislature, with a view to aid the collection of taxes, had determined to take tobacco in lieu of specie in the payment of taxes at a price to be determined by the executive, but not to exceed 28 shillings. This proposition was accepted by the moderate members in the hope of preventing worse measures — like the issue of more paper money.